Stoic Training

EPICTETUS' DISCOURES BOOK 3

STOICISM IN PLAIN ENGLISH

Dr. Chuck Chakrapani

THE STOIC GYM PUBLICATIONS

Stoic Gym Publications
www.thestoicgym.com

Ordering Information:
Quantity sales. Special discounts are available on quantity pur-
chases by corporations, associations, and others. For details,
contact the "Special Sales Department" at the address above.

Stoic Foundations/Chuck Chakrapani. —1st ed.
ISBNs:
Print: 978-0-920219-32-4
ePub: 978-0-920219-33-1
Mobi: 978-0-920219-34-8
PDF: 978-0-920219-35-5
17 18 19 20 21 22 23 24 25 26   1 2 3 4 5 6 7 8 9 0

Contents

Stoic Training

This is the third book of Epictetus' Discourses. In the first book, *Stoic Foundations*, Epictetus discusses the basic themes of Stoicism. In his second book, *Stoic Choices*, he discusses what a Stoic should do when faced with choices in different contexts

In this third book, *Stoic Training*, Epictetus talks about how Stoics may progress in their training.

Stoic Training: A quick outline

Like the first two books, *Stoic Training* revolves around a limited number of themes. These themes are reprised not only in this book, but in other (Discourses) books as well. These are some of the basic disciplines discussed in this book:

1. *Stoic training aims to make you excellent as a human being.* What makes a horse or a lion excellent does not make a human being excellent. For human beings

to be excellent, they should excel in their choices. When you start training, keep away from temptations, and keep the right company until your mind gets strong. [1, 12, 16]

2. *Stoic training consists of three disciplines: desire, action, and assent.*

    a. *Dealing with desires and aversions [the Discipline of Desire]*: To always get what you desire and never get what you want to avoid.

    b. *Dealing with choices to act or not to act [The discipline of action]*: To always act appropriately. Not to act carelessly but in an orderly fashion after due consideration.

    c. *Dealing with judgment [The discipline of assent]*: To avoid error and hasty judgment. [2, 12]

3. *Stoic training consists only of dealing with one's choices.* Train yourself to ignore and not judge whatever is not your choice. The final aim is to assent to what is true, dissent from what is false, and suspend judgment when uncertain; similarly, to desire what is good, to reject what is bad, and be indifferent to what is neither. [3]

4. *Train your mind to want whatever actually happens.* This way you'll never be disappointed no matter what happens. Keep your goals always in mind. Train yourself daily to deal with impressions. It is our judgement that decides whether what happens to us is good or bad. Make sure that your judgments are sound. [4, 5, 8, 9]

5. *Stoic training means to prepare ourselves for the challenges to come.* Illness and death are part of reality. There is no occasion for anger or fear. You are not desolate merely because you are alone, any more than you are secure from desolation because you are in a crowd. Train to be self-sufficient and be comfortable with yourself as well as with others. [10, 13]

6. *Ascetic training is unnecessary unless it serves some purpose.* Avoid unnecessarily harsh training. Practice getting rid of diffidence and conceit. If you decide to pursue anything, make sure you are prepared to do what it takes. Not everyone is cut out to do everything. [14, 15]

7. *Train to see things as they are without adding your judgements to them.* When you see things like poverty, don't add your judgment to it that it is bad. If you see people who have what you don't have, don't envy them. They paid a price for what they have. [17]

8. *Your judgements are the sole cause of your distress, because nothing outside of you can harm you.* You can spot an advantage even in things others consider 'bad', such as illness and death. [18, 19, 20]

9. *Don't imitate others without understanding the basis of their actions.* You should first master the principles. Approach things with caution and respect. Be aware of your limitations. Show your mastery by the way you act and not by blindly imitating others. [21]

10. *Train to be at home wherever you are.* Things are impermanent. Don't long for the past. Train yourself to be at home wherever you are and whoever you are

with. Do what needs doing and don't complain. This is where happiness is. It is impossible to be happy and yet crave what you don't have. Happiness must already have all it wants. It must resemble a person who has achieved their fill, feeling neither hungry nor thirsty. [24]

11. *Your goal is happiness and good fortune.* Never be beaten. If you don't achieve it at one attempt, try again and again. But don't make failure a habit. [25]

12. *Confront your fear of death.* You will see it is the fear of death rather than death that is the cause of your problem. [25, 26]

References

- The numbers in square brackets in this section refer to the discourse number.
- The letters after specific quotes in the book refer to the translators. They also happen to be the sources I relied on most often.
  - [WO] William A. Oldfather
  - [RD] Robert Dobbin, Penguin Classics
  - [CG/RH] Christopher Gill (ed.)/Robin Hard, Everyman
  - [RH] Robin Hard, Oxford World's Classics
  - [GL] George Long, Delphi Classics
- Any other text in square brackets is not part of the original text, but inserted by me for clarification or as a commentary. I have chosen this method to avoid

STOIC TRAINING • 5

readers going back and forth between the text and end notes.

- The first and last sections (*Key ideas of this discourse* and *Think about this*) are set in italics to remind readers that they are not a part of the original text but are added by me to reinforce the ideas of the discourse. All headings and subheadings are also inserted by me, so the material is easy to follow.

Your Choices
Shape Your Excellence

Key ideas of this discourse

1. *What makes an animal excellent does not make a human being excellent.*

2. *Your superiority as a human being comes from your ability to reason.*

3. *Adorn yourself as befits a human being.*

4. *Your beauty comes from the nature of your choices.*

The excellence of an animal
is not the excellence of a human

A richly dressed rhetoric student with an elaborate hair style came to Epictetus. Epictetus asked the student:

"Tell me, don't you think that some dogs and horses are beautiful? And, in general, is this not true of all animals?"

"Yes, it is."

"Is this also not true of human beings – some are beautiful, others ugly?"

"Of course."

"Do we call an animal beautiful because it is beautiful in a general sort of way or because it is beautiful in a specific way? For example, a dog is born for one thing and a horse for another, and a nightingale for yet another. Each one is beautiful when it fulfils its function, its own nature. But the nature of each is different, so each must be beautiful in a different way. Do you agree?"

"I suppose so."

"I imagine that what makes a pentathlete look good would not make a wrestler look good. It may even make a runner look absurd. The qualities that make a pentathlete look beautiful may make a wrestler look ugly."

"Very true."

"Then, is what makes a man beautiful the same as what makes a dog or a horse beautiful in its kind?"

"Yes."

"Then, what makes a dog beautiful?"

"Its excellence as a dog."

"What makes a horse beautiful?"

"Its excellence as a horse."

"What makes a human being beautiful? Shouldn't it be the excellence of a human being? So, young man, if you want to appear beautiful, you should strive for the excellence of a human being."

"And what might that be?"

"When you praise people in an unbiased way, who do you praise: the just or the unjust?"

"The just."

"The moderate or those who indulge in excess?"

"The moderate."

"The restrained or the unrestrained?"

"The restrained."

"If you make yourself such a person, you can be sure that you make yourself beautiful. If you neglect these things, no matter what you do to make yourself appear beautiful, you will necessarily be ugly."

Beyond that, I don't know what I can tell you. If I say anything more, I will hurt your feelings, and you will go away, perhaps never to return. But if I don't say anything, consider my behaviour: You come to me hoping you would gain some improvement and I bring you none. You come to me as a philosopher and I don't act like one. Besides how is it not cruel on my part not to correct you? Should you come to your senses sometime in the future, you'll have good reason to accuse me:

"Epictetus saw me in such a disgraceful condition and yet didn't say a word. What did he observe in me that he left me as I was? Did he despair of me so much? Was I not young? Was I not ready to listen to reason? Aren't there many other young people who make many such mistakes at their age? I have heard of one Polemo who was depraved in his youth and yet changed totally later. Maybe Epictetus didn't think I could be a Polemo; but he could at least have straightened my hair, stripped me of my ornaments, and prevented me from plucking my hairs from my body. Even though he saw me looking like – what shall I say? – he kept quiet."

Exceptional beings are different from the rest

For my part, I won't say what you look like. But, when you come to your senses, *you* will realize what it is and what kind of people behave this way. If you accuse me someday, how will I defend myself? Yes, but what if I speak and you don't pay any attention? Did Laius pay any attention to Apollo? [Apollo told Laius, who fathered Oedipus, that, if he had a son, the son would kill his father and marry his mother.] Did he not go away, get drunk, and dismiss the oracle from his mind? That did not stop Apollo telling him the truth. While I may have no idea if you would listen to me or not, Apollo knew perfectly well that Laius would pay no attention to him, and yet he spoke anyway.

"Why did he speak?"

Did Socrates succeed in persuading all who came to see him to take care of their character? No, not one in a thousand. Yet, as he has been appointed to this post by God (as he himself says), he never abandoned the post. What did he say to the judges?

"If you release me on condition that I should no longer act as I do now, I won't accept your offer. I won't stop acting the way I do now. I'll go up to the young and old – that is everyone I meet – and ask them the same questions I ask now. Above all, I will question you, my fellow citizens, because you are most closely related to me."

"Why are you so inquisitive and meddlesome, Socrates? What does it matter to you how we behave?"

"What are you saying? You are my companion and my relative. Yet you neglect yourself, provide the city a bad citizen, your relatives with a bad relative, and your neighbours with a bad neighbour."

"Why, who are you?"

"I am he whose duty it is to take care of human beings."

It is no small thing to be in a position to reply this way. When a lion comes along, no small ox dares to confront him. But if a bull comes forward to confront him, say to the bull – if you think fit – "Who are you?" or, "Why do you care?"

Man, in every species nature produces an exceptional being. Among cattle, among dogs, among bees, among horses. Don't ask that exceptional being, "Why, who are you?" If you do, it will, one way or another, find a voice that will tell you, "I am like the purple in the robe. Don't expect me to be like the rest. Don't find fault with my nature that made me different from the rest."

What then? Am I that kind of person? How could I be? How about you? Are you the kind of person who can listen to the truth? I wish you were.

Your superiority lies in your ability to reason

Nevertheless, because I am somehow condemned to wear a grey beard and rough cloak [philosopher's symbols], and because you came to me as to a philosopher, I will not treat you cruelly or act as though I am despaired of you. Instead, I will ask you: "Young man, whom do you wish to make beautiful?"

First learn who you are and then adorn yourself accordingly. You are a human being, a mortal animal, capable of using reason to evaluate impressions. What does it mean to use reason? In accordance with nature, and perfectly.

"In what way are you superior? Is it the animal in you?"

"No."

"Is it your mortality?"

"No."

"The ability to deal with impressions?"

"No."

"What makes you superior is your ability to reason. Decorate and beautify that aspect of you. Leave your hair to the creator to fashion the way he sees fit. What else? Are you a man or a woman?"

"A man."

"Then adorn yourself as man and not as a woman."

Adorn yourself appropriately

A woman is by nature smooth-skinned and delicate. If she's covered with hair she would be exhibited as an omen [according to the then prevailing customs]. The same applies to a man. A man devoid of hair would also be considered an omen. But if a man deliberately cuts it off or pulls it out, what can we make of him? How would we exhibit him? What can be we say about him: "A man who would rather be a woman?" How scandalous! Who would not be shocked by this? I do believe that even the men who pluck their hair do so without realizing that this is what they are doing.

Man, what complaint do you have against nature? That she made you a man? Should she have made everyone a woman? If that is the case, for whom would you make yourself beautiful? Does the whole thing displease you? Then go back and make a thorough job of it. Remove – how shall I put it – the cause of all this hairiness? Turn yourself completely into a woman, so we may have no doubt instead of this half-man half-woman thing.

"Who do you want to please? The women? Then please them as a man."

"But they like men with smooth bodies."

Go hang yourself. If they liked sexual perverts, would you become one? Is this your business in life? Is this what you were brought into this world for – to make yourself appealing to licentious women? Shall we make a man like you a citizen of Corinth, perhaps a city warden, or superintendent of young men, or army commander, or president of the games? Tell me, will you pluck your hair even when you're married? For whom? For what purpose? When you become a father, will you introduce your boys to the community with their hair plucked? Oh, what a fine citizen, what a fine senator, what a fine orator!

Is it young men of this kind that we should have born and raised among us? No, young man, by the gods let it not be your fate. Once you have heard these words, go home and tell yourself: "It wasn't Epictetus who told me all this. How could he have come up with this? It must be some benevolent god, speaking through him. It would have never entered his mind to say such things, because he is not in the habit of speaking to anyone. Well, let's obey God then and not incur his anger."

If a raven gives you a sign through croaking, it isn't the raven but the god speaking through him. If the god gives a sign through a human voice, will you pretend that it is simply a human being who is saying this to you and fail to recognize the divine voice? Will you not recognize that he gives signs to some people one way, and to other people another way? And, when it comes to the highest and most important matters, he gives the sign through his noblest messenger? What else does the poet mean when he says:

"...since we ourselves warned him,
By sending keen-sighted Hermes, the slayer of Argus,
Neither to murder the man, nor make love to his wife."

[Translation by CG/RH]

Just as Hermes came down to tell these things to Odysseus, so now the god is telling you the same by sending Hermes [in the form of Epictetus] not to distort what is already right: Let a man be a man, let a woman be a woman, let a beautiful human being be beautiful as a human being, and an ugly human being be ugly as a human being. You are not flesh or hair but what you choose. If you make that beautiful, then you will be beautiful.

Your beauty comes from the nature of your choices

So far, I haven't had the courage to tell you that you are ugly since I believe that you'd rather not hear it. But consider what Socrates said to the most beautiful and attractive of all men, Alcibiades: "Try, then, be beautiful." What did he mean by it? "Curl your locks and pluck hair from your legs?" Heaven forbid! No, he meant, "Make your choices beautiful. Get rid of wrong judgments."

"How to treat the poor body, then?"

"Leave it to nature. Someone else takes care of that. Leave it to them."

"Let my body be dirty, then?"

"By no means. Clean your body in accordance with your nature so that a man is clean as a man, a woman as a woman, and a child as a child. Otherwise, we might pluck out a lion's mane, so he may not be left 'dirty.' And the cock's comb as well, since he too needs to be 'clean.' Yes, he should be, but a cock as a cock, a lion as a lion, and the hound as a hound."

Think about this

Make beautiful your moral purpose, eradicate your worthless opinions. Socrates. Discourses III.1.42. Epictetus [WO]

DISCOURSE 2

The Three Aspects of Stoic Training

Key ideas of this discourse

1. *Stoic practices fall into three areas: desire, action, and assent.*
2. *Of these the most important and urgent is to deal with our desire. We should always be able to get what we want and always be able to avoid what we don't want.*
3. *We cannot deal with wrong judgments (assent) if we are not in control of our desires (desire) and actions (action).*

Three fields of study

If you want to be noble and good, you need to train yourself in three areas:

1. *Dealing with desires and aversions*: To always get what you desire and never get what you want to avoid. [The discipline of desire]

2. *Dealing with choices to act or not to act:* To always act appropriately. Not to act carelessly but in an orderly fashion after due consideration. [The discipline of action]
3. *Dealing with judgment:* To avoid error and hasty judgment. [The discipline of assent]

Why they are important

Of these three, the most important and urgent is the first one – dealing with our passions. Passions arise only when we are frustrated in our desires or faced with what we don't want. It is this that introduces confusion, turmoil, misfortunes, and calamities. It causes sorrows, grief, and envy; and it makes us envious and jealous. These passions make us incapable of listening to reason.

The second discipline (action) is concerned with acting the right way. I should not be unfeeling like a statue but should take care of my natural and acquired relationships – as a human being who honours gods, as a son, as a brother, as a father, as a citizen.

The third (assent) belongs to those already making progress. It is concerned with achieving certainty in the matters already covered, even while we are asleep, drunk, or depressed. No untested impression can catch us off-guard. Some argue that this is beyond us. But that's because philosophers these days neglect the first two areas and concentrate on the third, concentrating upon equivocal arguments, and arguments developed through questioning and those that are fallacious, like *"The Liar."*

"True, but it is because we need to protect ourselves against being deceived when dealing with these matters."

"Who needs to? Only the person who is already excellent and good."

Is it only in this regard you fall short? Have you mastered other subjects? Aren't you liable to be deceived when handling money? When you see a pretty girl, can you resist the impression? Don't you feel a tinge of envy when your neighbour receives an inheritance? Is proper judgment the only thing you lack? Poor man, even while you are studying all this, you are fearful and anxious at the thought that someone may despise you and ask whether anyone has said anything about you.

We don't value our choices and look for outside approval

If someone should come and tell you that, "When discussing philosophers, someone said that you were the one true philosopher," your little soul grows from an inch to a yard. But if someone else who was there should say, "Nonsense. He is not worth listening to. It is a waste of time. What does he know? He has the basics, nothing more," you are distraught. You turn pale and cry out, "I'll show him what sort of a man I am. I am a great philosopher!" But this very behaviour shows what you are. Why do you pretend it to be something else? Don't you know that [the Cynic philosopher] Diogenes showed up a sophist that way, by pointing at him with his middle finger? [a rude gesture] When the man became furious with rage, Diogenes said, "That is the man. I have pointed out him to you." A human being is not like a stone or a stick, to be shown by pointing one's finger. But when a person shows what his judgments are, then he has shown what he is as a human being.

Let us look at your judgments, too. Is it not clear that you place no value on your own choices but look beyond them – what someone else will say, what someone else will think of you, whether they will think that you are a scholar, whether you have read [the Stoic philosophers] Chrysippus and Antipater? Well, if you have read [the Stoic philosopher] Archedemus too, you have everything! Why are you still worried that you may fail in showing us who you are? Will you let me tell you what you have shown yourself to be? A person who comes before us mean, hypocritical, quick-tempered, and cowardly; finding fault with everything, blaming everybody, never at peace, and arrogant – this is what you have shown us.

Go away now and read Archedemus; then, if a mouse falls and makes a noise, you will die of fright! Like it happened to – what was his name? – oh yes, Crinis, who also prided himself on understanding Archedemus. [Crinis was a not-so-prominent Stoic philosopher who was supposed to have died by a stroke caused by fright at a mouse falling from a wall.]

The discipline of assent belongs only to those who are already at peace

Idiot, why don't you leave things that don't concern you alone? They are suitable only for those who can learn from them with an undisturbed mind and truly say, "I don't give in to anger, sorrow or envy. I am free of restraint and compulsion. What do I lack? I am at leisure, I have peace of mind. Let's now deal with equivocal arguments. Let's see how one may adopt a hypothesis and yet may never come to an absurd conclusion."

These things belong to people of that type. Those who are safe may light a fire, dine and, if they please, even sing and dance. But you are coming to me when your ship is already sinking. You are now starting to hoist topsails!

Think about this

[Passions] are produced in no other way than by the disappointment of our desires, and the incurring of aversions.
Discourses III.2.2 Epictetus [CG/RH]

The Main Objective of Stoic Training

Key ideas of this discourse

1. Impressions are the raw material we need to work with.
2. By nature, we gravitate towards what is good and move away from what is bad.
3. Our only concern is about our choices. Good and bad arise out of our choices and others have nothing to do with it.
4. If you are interested in getting something from others, you need to give them what they want.
5. This is how you train yourself. Throughout the day observe people and situations. Some of these may strike you as fortunate and others as unfortunate. Test each situation by this criterion: "Is this situation the result your choice?" If the answer is no, then it is none of your concern. Your judgments in such situations are mere opinions with no substance.

6. *Just as a ray of light is not disturbed when its reflection in water is disturbed, your knowledge and virtues are not disturbed when your soul appears disturbed..*

Impressions are our raw material to work with

The human body is the raw material for the physician and physiotherapist. Land is the raw material for the farmer. The raw material for good human beings is their own mind – to respond to impressions the way intended by nature. How did nature intend? To assent to what is true, dissent from what is false, and suspend judgment when uncertain; similarly, to desire what is good, to reject what is bad, and be indifferent to what is neither.

Your soul gravitates toward good and recoils from bad

A banker or a retailer cannot refuse to accept legal currency. They are obliged to accept it, whether they like it or not, in exchange for goods of equal value. So it is with the soul. When you present it with something good, it immediately moves towards it and it is repelled by anything bad. The soul will never reject a clear impression of good, any more than you would reject legal currency. Every action of God and humans is solely based on this principle. Good is preferred above every form of relationship.

"My father is nothing to me, only the good."

"Are you so unfeeling?"

"It's my nature. I am so designed by God. If good turns out to be something different from decency and fairness, then off go father, brother, country, and the rest. What! Am I supposed to give up my own good so you can have yours? Why?"

"Because I am your father."

"But not my good."

"Because I am your brother."

"But not my good."

On the other hand, if we place our good in right choice, then maintaining such relationships also becomes good. Anyone who gives up some material things also attains good.

"My father is wasting my inheritance."

"But he is not harming you."

"My brother will get a bigger inheritance."

"Let him take as much as he likes."

Will he take a greater share of honesty, loyalty, and brotherly love? No. Not even God can do that. He placed my good nature in my power and gave it to me, as he has it himself – free, clear, and without restrictions.

To get what you want, offer others what they want

Different people may use different currencies. If you pay them in their currency, what they sell can be yours.

- A corrupt person comes to power. What currency does he recognize? Money. Show him the money and you can carry off what you please.
- You face an adulterer. What currency does he recognize? Pretty girls. Offer the right currency and get what you want.
- Another is addicted to boys. Give him his currency.
- Another is fond of hunting. Give her a handsome horse or dog. She may groan and complain but will have an inner compulsion to sell what you like for the currency you offer.

The basic training procedure

Here is how you train yourself. Go out early in the morning. Examine closely whomever you see or hear and consider what you have seen:

- A handsome man or a beautiful woman? Test them by your rule: Is their beauty within your choice? No? Forget them.
- Someone grieving for the death of a child? Apply the rule. Death is beyond your choice. Dismiss it from your mind.
- A consul met you? Apply the same rule. Is consulship inside or outside your choice? Outside. Throw that aside as well. It failed the test. Reject it. It is nothing to you.

If we practiced this way every day from morning to night, by God, we would see some results. As it is, though, we are half asleep and overcome by every impression we face. If we ever wake up, it is for a brief while in the lecture theatre. When we go out, if we see someone in distress we say, "He is crushed;" if we see a consul we say, "A lucky man;" if we see a poor woman, we say "How tragic! How is she going to get her next meal?"

Get rid of deceptive opinions

We must get rid of such deceptive opinions with all our strength.

What is misfortune? An opinion.

What is subversion, dissension, complaint, blame, accusation, or foolish talk? All mere opinions, things that are not subject to our choice.

If you transfer your opinions to what is within your choice, I guarantee you peace of mind, no matter what is happening around you.

Your knowledge and virtues are not affected by impressions

The soul is like a bowl filled with water. Impressions are like a ray of light that strikes the water. If the water is disturbed, the ray will seem to be disturbed as well, although it is not. So, when someone loses consciousness, her knowledge and virtues are not compromised, but the spirit in which they exist. Once the spirit returns to normal, so do knowledge and virtues.

Think about this

What, after all, are sighing and crying, except opinions?
What is 'misfortune'? An opinion. Discourses III.3.18. Epictetus [RD]

Train Your Mind to Want Whatever Happens

Key ideas of this discourse

1. *People imitate the behaviour of their superiors. So, if you are a powerful person, you should set an example for others by your behaviour.*
2. *When you wish for anything other than what actually happens, you put yourself in conflict with others who may wish otherwise.*
3. *Let your choice be in accordance with nature.*

The masses imitate their superiors

When the governor of Epirus expressed his support of a comic actor in an excessive way, he was abused in public for doing so. He was upset by the way he was treated and related this incident to Epictetus, expressing indignation. Epictetus asked,

"What did they do wrong? They were only showing excessive support the way you did."

"Is this the way, then, that people should express their support?"

"Yes, when they saw you, the governor, the friend and official of Caesar, display obvious partiality, naturally they assumed they could do so too. If it is inappropriate to be so partial, stop doing it yourself. If it is appropriate, why be upset if they imitate you?

Who are the masses going to imitate, if not you, their superior? Who are they going to look at when they come to the theatre, if not you?"

'Look how the governor behaves!'

'He is yelling. In that case, I can yell too.'

'He jumps from his seat. I will jump from my seat too.'

'His subordinates sit in different parts of the theatre and shout their applause. I don't have anyone to do that for me, but I will make up for it by shouting louder than all of them.'

You should serve as a model for others

You should know that when you go to the theatre you serve as a model. You set the standard of behaviour for others to follow. Why, then, did they abuse you? Because everyone hates what stands in their way. They wanted someone to win the accolade and you wanted someone else to win it. They were standing in your way and you in theirs. You turned out to be the stronger. They did what they could and ranted against what stood in their way. What do you expect? That *you* should be able to do whatever you wish but they should not even *say* what they wish?

And why are you surprised by any of this? Don't farmers blame God when they think he stands in their way? Isn't an emperor blamed all the time? What then? Don't think that they are unaware of it. The emperor's spies report to him whatever they overhear. How does he respond? He knows that if he punished everyone who ever said something bad about him, he would have no one left to rule over. What then?

Train yourself to wish for whatever happens

When you enter the theatre should you say, "Let so-and-so win the accolade"? No, you should say, "Let my choice be in accordance with nature. No one is dearer to me than myself. It would be absurd for me to harm myself so someone else can win the accolade as an actor."

"Whom then should I wish get the accolade?"

"The one who does. That way the person you want to win will always win."

"But I would rather have so-and-so get the accolade."

"Well then, hold as many contests at home as you like. Declare him to be the winner in all contests. Call him the Olympic winner. But, in public, don't claim more than your due. Don't steal what is public property. Otherwise the masses will abuse you. After all, if you act like them, you put yourself at their level."

Think about this

Every man hates what stands in his way. They wanted so-and-so to get the crown and you wanted the other man to get it...They did what they could and reviled what was standing in their way. What, then, do you wish? Discourses III.4.6. Epictetus [WO]

Avoid Excuses and Train Everyday

Key ideas of this discourse

1. *Sooner and later, illness and death will overtake us all.*
2. *So, instead of complaining, we should accept them cheerfully.*
3. *Aim to improve yourself every day.*

Stop complaining

A student says [to Epictetus]

"I am not well. I would like to go home."

"Were you never ill at home, then? Did you ever think about whether you are doing anything here that would improve the quality of choices you make? For, if you are not achieving anything, you might as well not have come here."

Go home. Take care of your household affairs. If your decision-making cannot be brought in line with nature, your little patch of land may. You may increase the amount of your small change, look after your father in his old age, wander around in the marketplace, and take up a job. Not being competent, you will do poorly whatever you happen to do next.

Keep your goals in mind

But, if you are aware that

- you are getting rid of your bad judgments and taking different ones in their place;
- you have changed your position from relying on things that lie outside the area of your choice to relying on those that are inside; and
- you sometimes cry, "Alas!" not for the sake of your father or brother, but for yourself,

then why pay attention to illness anymore? Don't you know disease and death will eventually overtake us, no matter what we are doing? If you think you can be doing something better than what you are doing here when you are overtaken, go and do it.

As far as I am concerned, when death finds me, I would rather be doing nothing other than taking care of things under the area of my choice – trying to make it unhindered, unrestrained, serene, and free. I want to be able to say to God,

"Have I in any way disobeyed your commands? Did I ever misuse the resources you gave me for any other purpose? Did I misuse my senses or my preconceptions? Did I ever accuse you of anything or find fault with the way you governed? I fell sick and it was your will. So did others, but I did it willingly. I became poor, it was your wish, but I was joyful. I didn't hold any office because it was not your wish, but I didn't set my heart on it. Have you ever seen me dejected because of it? Have I not always come before you with a cheerful face, prepared to do whatever you order me? Now it is your wish that I leave this festival. I go; full of gratitude to you that you found me worthy of sharing this festival with you; and see your works and the way you govern."

Let these be my thoughts, let this be my writing, and let this be my reading, when I face death.

"But my mother won't hold my head in her arms when I am sick."

"Go home to your mother then. You deserve to be sick and have someone hold your head."

"At home I have a nice bed to lie on."

"Go back to your bed, then. No doubt you deserve to lie on such a fine bed, even when healthy. Please do not miss out on, by being here, what you could be doing there."

Aim for improvement everyday

But what does Socrates say? "As one man rejoices in improving his farm and another his horse, so I rejoice day-by-day in following my own improvement."

"In what way? Little philosophical phrases?"

"Man, hold your tongue."

"In little philosophic theories, then?"

"What are you saying?"

"Well, I don't see anything else that philosophers spend their time on."

Does it mean nothing to you to never to accuse anyone, never to blame anyone, be it God or men? To always have the same expression in one's face, coming in or going out? These are things that Socrates knew. Yet he never said he knew. He didn't teach either. If anyone asked for philosophic phrases or theories, he would take them to Protagoras or Hippias [Sophists who taught rhetoric]. It was like taking someone over to the market, if they came looking for fresh vegetables. Who, among you, makes the purpose of Socrates the purpose of your life? If you did, you would be glad to be ill, to go hungry, or to die. If anyone of you has been in love with a pretty woman, you will know that I am telling the truth.

Think about this

I hope death overtakes me when I am occupied solely with the care of my character in order to make it passionless, free, unrestrained. Discourses III.5.7 Epictetus [RD]

Where You Train, There You Find Results

Key ideas of this discourse

1. Don't spend time on one thing and expect results elsewhere.

2. A good person restricts his or her decisions to what is under their control. Such a person is invincible.

3. People tend to gravitate towards their natural object.

Don't spend your efforts on one thing and expect results in another

Someone asked Epictetus:

"How it is that, although more and more people are devoted to logic these days, more progress was made in the past?"

"On what are we spending more effort now? In what was the progress great then?"

If we spend more time on something at present, we will also find more progress at present. People are spending more time these days studying syllogism, and in that there is progress. But, in the past, they spent more time in keeping their choices in accordance with nature and in that there was progress. Therefore, do not substitute one for the other. Don't spend your efforts on one thing and expect results in another. Rather, see if you can find a person who devotes his efforts to living their life keeping their choice in accordance with nature. Have they failed to make progress? You will not find anyone like that.

A good person cannot fail

A good person cannot be defeated. They do not enter into contests in which they are not superior. They say,

"If you want my country property, take it. Take my servants, take my office, and take my poor body. But you cannot stop me from getting what I want or force me to get what I don't want."

This is the only contest they would enter. How can they fail? How can they be defeated?

The meaning of "general perception"

"Epictetus, what is 'general perception'?"

"When you hear a sound, it is general hearing. But when you distinguish between musical notes, it is no longer 'general,' but technical. There are things that

people who are not altogether perverted can see because
of their general faculties. Such mental condition is called
'general perception.'"

We tend to gravitate
towards our natural object

It is not easy to succeed with young men who are soft –
you cannot hold soft cheese with a hook. But the gifted
people, even if you try to turn them away, hold on to reason even more firmly.

[Musonius] Rufus, for the most part, tried to turn
them away in order to distinguish the gifted from those
who are not. He used to say, "Just as it is with a stone
which, by virtue of its nature, falls to Earth even when
you throw it upwards, so it is with a gifted person. The
more you try to beat him off, the more he inclines towards his natural object."

Think about this

*Do not confuse different things, nor when you devote your
efforts to one thing, expect to make progress in another.*
Discourses III.6.4. Epictetus [CG/RH]

Pleasures of the Mind Are Superior to Bodily Pleasures

Key ideas of this discourse

1. *Three things belong to human beings: body, mind, and externals. Of these, mind is the best.*
2. *If mind is the best, then pleasures of the flesh must necessarily be inferior to it.*
3. *Therefore, Epicurus is wrong in saying that pleasures of the flesh are of primary importance.*
4. *By concentrating on pleasures of the flesh to the exclusion family and society, Epicurean philosophy advocates a society without ethics.*
5. *The flesh itself is not important. What the flesh does is.*

The mind is supreme

The commissioner, an Epicurean, visited Epictetus who said,

"Just as a person who arrived in a new city asks for directions from those who know the place, it is natural for laypeople like us to ask you what the best thing in the world is. When we have learned what it is, just as visitors do, we may seek it out and look at it. Three things belong to a human being: mind, body, and externals. Hardly anyone denies this. All you have to do is answer the question which is the best. What are we going to tell others? The flesh? And was it for the pleasure of the flesh that Maximus sailed in winter all the way to Cassiope with his son? [There were two prominent people by the name Maximus during Epictetus' time. It is unclear to which Maximus Epictetus was referring.]

"Of course not."

"Isn't it proper, then, to pay attention to what is best in us?"

"It is."

"What do we have that is better than the flesh?"

"The mind."

"Which is better: things of the best part or things of the inferior parts?"

"Things of the best."

"Does the pleasure of the mind lie within the area of our choice?"

"It does."

"How does this pleasure arise? By itself? That can't be. For we must assume that the essence of good has been in existence prior to this and we feel the pleasure when we partake of it."

"Yes."

What, then, triggers the pleasure in our mind? If it relates to the mind, the essence of the good has been found.
It is impossible that the good should be one thing and our
delight should come from something else – it is claiming
that the effect is good, while the cause is not. If the effect
is good, the cause must be good. But, if you have any
sense, you should not admit to this; It would be inconsistent with Epicurus and the other doctrines of your
school. All that you can say is that pleasure of the mind
is the pleasure of the bodily things. They are now of primary value and are essentially good. Maximus was foolish to undertake the voyage if his purpose was anything
other than the flesh, since that is the best. He is also foolish if he fails to take what belongs to another when he
can do so as a judge.

The reason to be good
should not be fear of being caught

But let's consider just this, if you please: How to do it secretly and safely so no will find out? After all, Epicurus
himself did not say that stealing is evil, but only being
found out. He says, "Do not steal," only because it is impossible to be sure that you won't be found out. But, let
me tell you, it is possible to escape detection if you steal
skilfully and cautiously. Besides, we have powerful
friends – both men and women – in high places. The
Greeks are too feeble to go to the top to complain. Why
do you not, then, go after what you believe to be good? It
is madness, it is stupidity. But if you tell me that you do

refrain, I would not believe you anyway. Just as it is impossible to agree to what is false or to deny what is clearly true, it is impossible not to go after what is good.

Now, wealth is good; it is the chief means by which you secure pleasure. Why don't you acquire it? And why don't you seduce the spouse of your neighbour if you can do it secretly? And break the neck of the other spouse too if you are found out? That is what you should do if you are consistent as a philosopher of your own doctrines. Otherwise, you are no different from us Stoics. You see, we too talk one thing and do another. We talk well, but act shamefully. But you are perversely different. You talk shamefully, but act well.

By God, can you imagine a country full of Epicureans? [If we did, conversations would go like this.]

"I shall not marry."

"Neither will I. We ought not to marry."

"Yes, we should not have children either."

"We should not engage in public affairs."

What is the result of all this? Where will the citizens come from? Who will educate them? Who will guide the young people? Who will train them to be athletes? What will they be taught? How do we decide this? Bring up a young person according to your doctrines. Your doctrines are bad, subversive of the state, destructive of the family, not even fit for women. [This is a strange comment coming from a Stoic. If 'goods of the mind' are the best, why would they be any different for women compared to men? It is obvious that the principles expounded by Epictetus apply to all human beings

STOIC TRAINING • 45

irrespective of gender. So it is unclear what Epictetus was trying to imply here. A misogynist insult accepted as normal during the times he lived? We can only speculate.]

Give them up, man. You live in an imperial city. It is your duty to hold office, judge the right way and keep your hands off the property of others. No other person except your spouse should seem beautiful to you. Not any other person, not even a plate of gold or silver. Look for doctrines that are consistent with such behaviour and you will gladly stay away from things that are persuasive enough to attract and overpower you. If we add to this the philosophy we just discovered, to help push us towards them and encourage us to do so, what will be the result?

Flesh is not important; the actions of the flesh are

Let's take a plate. What is best, the silver or the workmanship? Hands may be made of flesh but what is important is the way they work. There are three kinds of appropriate actions:

1. Actions that relate to mere existence;
2. Actions that relate to existence of a particular kind; and
3. Actions that are our principal duties.

So it is with human beings. we should not honour the material itself which is the flesh but its principal duties. What are they? Involvement in public affairs, marriage, procreation, worship of the divine, and caring for parents. In general, having desire and aversion and having impulse to act or not act, depending on whether it is in accordance with nature.

"What is in accordance with nature?"

"To be free, as noble and self-respecting."

After all, what other animal blushes? What other animal has a sense of shame? It is our nature to subject pleasure to these considerations as their servant. This will arouse our interest in continuing to act in accordance with nature.

"But I am rich. I need nothing."

"Then why do you pretend to be a philosopher? Your gold and silver plates are enough for you. What do you need doctrines for?"

"I am also the judge of the Greeks."

"Do you know how to judge? Who taught you that?"

"Caesar wrote me testimonials."

"Let him write you testimonials that will allow you to judge music and literature. What good will it do you? Let me ask you another question. How did you become a judge? Whose hand did you kiss? That of [influential freedman] Symphorous or of Numenius? In front of whose bedroom door did you sleep [so you can salute him as soon as he wakes up]? To whom did you send presents? Don't you see that the office of judge is worth no more than what Numenius is worth?"

"But I can throw anyone I want in prison."

"As you can a stone."

"But I can club anyone to death."

"As you can a donkey."

This is not governing people. Govern us as rational human beings. Show us what is in our interest and we will follow that. Show us what is not in our interest and we will avoid that. Like Socrates, make us admire and imitate you. He was one person who governed people as human beings – he caused people to subject to him their desires and aversions and their impulses to act or not to act. "Do this; don't do that or I will send you to prison" is not the way to govern people as rational beings. No. What you should be saying is

"Do this in accordance with nature, or you will be punished, you will be harmed."

"Harmed in what way?"

"Only in this way: You will destroy yourself as a person of good faith, honour and decent behaviour. Look for no greater harm than that."

Think about this

The substance of a hand is flesh, but its operations are the principal things. Discourses II.7.24. Epictetus [CH/RH]

DISCOURSE 8

Train to Deal with Impressions

Key ideas of this discourse

1. *Train every day to deal with impressions*
2. *Good and bad comes from your choices. What you don't have control over is neither good nor bad.*
3. *If you judge every impression by this criterion, you will see progress.*

Training to deal with everyday impressions

Just as we train ourselves to answer obscure, nit-picking questions, so should we train to deal with everyday impressions because they implicitly question us. You should be able to answer those questions as follows:

"So-and-so's son died. What do you think of that?"

"That's not something he can control. So, it is not bad."

"So-and-so's father left him nothing when he died."

49

"The son cannot control his father's actions. So, it is not bad."

"He was condemned by the authorities."

"Outside his control. So, it is not bad."

"He is distressed by all this."

"This is under his control. So, it is bad."

"He faced it with dignity."

"This is under his control. So, it is good."

If you make dealing with impressions a habit, you'll make progress. You will not accept anything as true, unless the impression so convinces you.

"His son is dead."

"What happened?"

"His son is dead."

"Nothing more?"

"Nothing more."

"The ship is lost."

"What happened?"

"The ship is lost."

"He was taken to prison."

"What happened?"

"He was taken to prison."

"It is too bad for him," is a comment that we add on our own. Yet, you may say, God is being unfair in all this. How so? Because he made you patient and high-minded? Because he prevented these things from being evil?

Because he made it possible for you to suffer and still be happy? Or because he left the door open for you to use when what happens doesn't suit you? Go out, friend, and stop complaining.

If you want to know what Romans think of philosophers, listen to this. Italicus, who had the reputation of being one of the finest philosophers, was angry with his friends when I was around. He said, "I can't stand it anymore. You're killing me. I will end up like him," – pointing to me!

Think about this

We should exercise ourselves daily to deal with impressions. Discourses III.8.1. Epictetus [CG/RH]

Train to Restrain Your Desires

Key ideas of this discourse

1. We constantly go after honours, but pay little attention to the nature of our judgements.
2. Constantly craving for more and more things leads to constant dissatisfaction.
3. The way out is to drop a few of your desires. Then you will get what you want.

We constantly go after greater honours

A man on his way to Rome came to see Epictetus. The man was engaged in a lawsuit regarding the honour to be bestowed upon him as a patron of a city. He described his situation to Epictetus and asked him what he thought of the matter. Epictetus said:

"If you are asking me what you will do in Rome and whether you will win or lose your case, I have nothing to say to you. But if are asking me how you will do, I can tell you that. If your judgments are right, you will do well; if they are wrong, you will not do well. How a person does depends on their judgment. Every time. Why are you so eager to get elected to this office? Your judgment. What makes you go to Rome? Your judgment. And risking wintry weather and spending your own money too. Why?"

"Because it is necessary."

"What makes you think that? Your judgment."

Therefore, if judgements are the causes of your actions, when your judgements are bad, the results will be bad – corresponding to the cause. Well then, are your judgments sound – both yours and your opponent's? If so, why do you disagree? Do you think that you are right and he is not? Why? Because you think so. But so does he. And so do crazy people. This is a bad criterion to go by.

But we don't stop to examine the nature of our judgements

But show me that you have examined your judgments carefully. You are not content to stay home with the honours you have already received, and you travel to Rome in order to receive the new honour of becoming a patron of the city. You desire something greater and more prominent. So, tell me, have you ever been on a journey to examine your own judgements, so you can reject those that are unsound? Whom did you consult for that purpose? What time have you set aside for this? In what stage of your life? Run through those periods in your life. Do it in your mind, if you are ashamed to do it in front of me.

- Did you examine your life when you were a child? Isn't it true that what you were doing then was not different from what you are doing now?

- Did you examine your life when you were a young person? When you listened to those who taught rhetoric and practised it yourself, did you imagine that you were deficient in anything?

- Did you examine your life when you became a man and took part in public affairs? When you pleaded cases yourself and acquired a reputation, did you imagine anyone else could be your equal? Would you have tolerated it if someone tried to cross-examine you, to show that your judgments were bad?

"Help me with this."

"I have no rules to offer you on this. If you have come to me for that purpose, you should have come here intending to meet a philosopher rather than a greengrocer or a shoemaker, as you have done now."

"For what purpose, then, do philosophers offer rules?"

"For this purpose: Whatever happens, our ruling faculty continues to be in accordance with nature. Does this seem small to you?"

"No. It's of the greatest importance."

"Well, can that be completed in a short time, in a brief visit? If it can be so completed, do so. And then you will go away and complain, 'I met Epictetus, but it was like meeting with a stone or a statue.' Yes, you simply saw me, nothing more."

You know someone only when you understand the nature of their judgements

You meet someone properly as a person only when you understand his judgments and show him yours in turn. Discover my judgments, show me yours, and then you can say you have met me. Let us cross-examine each other. If any of my judgements is bad, take it away; if any of yours is bad, let's bring it to light. This is what meeting a philosopher is all about.

But no, this is your way: "We were passing through. And, while we were waiting to charter a ship to go to Rome, we thought we could visit Epictetus to see what he has to say." Then you leave saying, "Epictetus was nothing at all. He murdered the language and spoke utter nonsense." What else could you judge, if you came here like this?

"But if I turn to these matters, I won't own land any more than you do. I won't own silver goblets any more than you do. And I won't own fine cattle any more than you do."

Constantly craving for more makes you dissatisfied with life

It is enough for me to respond this way:

"But I have no need for such things. For you, even if you acquire more things, you'll need even more. Whether you wish it not, you are poorer than I am."

"What do you need, then?"

"Things you don't have now: stability, a mind in accord with nature, and freedom from tension. Patron or no patron, what do I care? But *you* do. I am richer than you are. I am not anxious about what Caesar will think of me. I flatter no one for that purpose. This is what I have instead of your plates of gold and silver."

You may own gold wares, but your reasoning, your judgments and assent, your impulses and desires are earthenware. When I have all these in accord with nature, why shouldn't I devote some time to the art of reasoning? I have leisure and my mind isn't distracted. What could I better be doing than this as a human being? You have nothing to do and you are restless. You go to the theatre and wander aimlessly.

Why shouldn't a philosopher cultivate his reason? You have fine crystal vases, I have the argument of *The Liar*. You have fine glassware and I the argument of the *Denyer*. [We have already discussed *The Liar* paradox in *Stoic Choices*. Chrysippus wrote two works on the *Denyer* argument, although scholars aren't sure about the nature of this argument.] To you, all you have seems small. To me, all I have seems important. Your desires cannot be fulfilled. Mine already are. When children put their hands into narrow-necked jar to get nuts and figs out, the same thing happens. Once they fill their hand, they cannot get it out. They cry. Drop a few and you will easily get it out. You too should drop your desires. Don't set your heart upon too many things and you'll get what you want.

Think about this

Everything you already have seems small in your sight but everything that I have seems important to me. Discourses III.9.21. Epictetus [WO]

Train to Deal with Illness

Key ideas of this discourse

1. *The purpose of training is to prepare you to face hardships, including illness.*
2. *Illness is a part of life. We should have our judgements ready and available to us when we need them – as when we get sick.*
3. *You should always keep two principles ready at hand:*
   a. *There is nothing good or bad, if it is outside your choice; and*
   b. *We should follow events rather than guide them.*

Review every day at bedtime

We should have our judgements ready and available to us when we need them: at lunch, our judgments about lunch; at the bath, our judgments about a bath; in bed, our judgments about a bed.

Let not sleep descend your weary eyes,
Before having reviewed every action of the day

Where did I go wrong? What did I do? What duty leave undone?

Starting here, review your actions, and afterwards,

Blame yourself for what is badly done and rejoice in the good.

[*The* Golden Verses, *attributed to Pythagoras. Translation by Robin Hard*]

We should keep these verses handy and put them to practical use and not as simple exclamations.

What to do when illness strikes

When fever strikes, we should have the judgments at hand and apply them. When you fall ill, don't forget and don't give up, saying, "If I ever study philosophy again, let things happen as they will. I will have to go somewhere and take care of my poor body." Yes indeed – if the fever doesn't go there with you!

But what does training in philosophy mean? Is it not to prepare yourself for the challenges to come? Don't you understand then, that what you are saying amounts to this: 'If I ever again prepare to bear quietly the things that happen to me, *then* let things happen as they will'? It is like someone withdrawing from the sports regimen because he has received some injuries. The only difference is that with sports regimen one may stop it to avoid further injuries. But if we stop training in philosophy, what good would it do? What should a philosopher say when facing any hardship in life? "It is for this hardship I have been training myself. It is for this I have been practicing."

STOIC TRAINING • 61

The purpose of training is to bear hardships well

God tells you: "Give me proof that you have competed according to the rules, followed the proper diet, exercised, and paid attention to your trainer." And then when the time for action comes, do you weaken? Now is the time for your fever. Bear it well. Thirsty? Bear it well. Hungry? Bear it well. Isn't this within your power? Who can stop you? Yes, your doctor may ask you not to drink, but he can't stop you from bearing thirst well. He can ask you not to eat, but he can't stop you from bearing hunger well.

"But, am I not a scholar."

"What are you studying for? Isn't it to be happy, idiot? Isn't it to be secure? Isn't it to live your life in conformity with nature? What prevents you, then, when you fall sick, from keeping your judgements in conformity with nature?"

Illness is a part of life

Here is the proof, the test for a philosopher. Fever is a part of life, just like a walk, a voyage, or a journey is. You don't read while taking a stroll, do you? No, no more than when you have a fever. But if you walk the right way, you are fulfilling your role as a walker. Similarly, if you bear your fever the right way then you are fulfilling your role as a patient.

"What does it mean to bear your fever, 'the right way'?"

"It is not to blame God or humans. It is not to be overwhelmed by what is happening. It is to await death courageously and in a becoming way. It is to do what you are instructed to do."

The universe will not be upset when you die

When your doctor comes, don't be worried about what he might say. Don't get carried away with joy if says, "You are doing very well." What is *good* about it? When you were well, what good was it to you? Similarly, don't be downhearted if he says, "You are in a bad way." What does it mean to be in a bad way? That your body and soul will separate soon? What is terrible about that? If you are not close to it now, will you not be close to it sometime in the future?

Is the universe going to be upset when you die? Why do you flatter your doctor, then? Why do say, "If you so wish, doctor, I will get well." Why do you give him an opportunity to exhibit his vanity? Why not just pay him his due – just as you would pay a shoemaker regarding your feet, a builder with regard to your house? Your body is not yours – it is something dead by nature. These are the things required of someone suffering from fever. If you fulfil these, you have what rightly belongs to you.

STOIC TRAINING • 63

Your training

"It isn't your job as a philosopher to safeguard the external things – not your wine, or oil, or your poor body."

"What, then?"

"Your governing principle."

"How about external things?"

"Only to the extent that you don't act thoughtlessly about them."

What occasion is left to be fearful, then? What occasion is left to be angry? Or to be afraid of things that are not your concern – worthless external things?

Two basic principles

These then are the two principles that you should always have ready at hand:

There is nothing good or bad, if it is outside your choice; and

We should follow events as they happen rather than guide them.

"My brother shouldn't have treated me this way."

"Quite so. But it is for him to see to that. No matter how he treats you, you need to conduct yourself the right way towards him. This is your business and not the rest. This no one can stop you from doing, while the other is open to hindrance.

Think about this

What occasion is there for fear? What occasion for anger, about things that are not our own and are of no value? Discourses III.10.17. Epictetus [CG/RH]

Remind Yourself of the Basic Principles

Key ideas of this discourse

1. *Whoever regards things that are not under their choice as good will be subject to envy and desire. They will flatter others and will be troubled.*
2. *Whoever regards things that are not under their choice as evil shall be full of sorrow, will grieve, will lament, and will be unhappy.*
3. *Everything comes from God. So, in all your personal and social relationships, do not dishonour others.*

Violating these principles will result in unhappiness

When we don't obey some rules, 'punishment' follows, as though we have disobeyed the divine governing order:

- Whoever regards things that are not under their choice as good will be subject to envy and desire. They will flatter others and shall be troubled.
- Whoever regards things that are not under their choice as evil will be full of sorrow, will grieve, will lament, and will be unhappy.

Yet, despite these harsh penalties, we cannot stop thinking this way.

Remember what the poet says of the stranger:

Stranger, it is not permitted, even if worse should come
Than you, to dishonour a stranger; for all come from
Zeus.

Strangers and beggars.

[This verse is frequently attributed to Homer in his *Odyssey*. The translation is by Robin Hard.]

You should also keep this thought at hand and apply it to your father, too: "I'm not permitted to dishonour you, father, even if I face something worse than you, because all things come from God, who protects parents." Likewise, in the case of a brother: "Because all things come from God of kindred." And in a similar manner in all our other relationships: We shall find God to be the overseer of them all.

Think about this

There are certain punishments laid down, as though by law, for those who disobey the divine governance. Discourses III.11.1 Epictetus [CG/RH]

Train Yourself in Three Areas of Study

Key ideas of this discourse

1. *Not everything that is difficult is suitable for training. We should train hard on things that are important to us.*
2. *Training should be tailored for each person, depending on where they are weak now.*
3. *The three areas of training are: Desires and aversions; impulse to act or not to act; and evaluating impressions before giving assent.*
4. *All useful training should be directed to these areas. Training directed towards externals is not our concern.*

Not everything that is difficult is suitable for training

We should not train ourselves using unnatural or strange practices. Otherwise, those of us who call ourselves philosophers will be no better than showmen. It is difficult and dangerous to walk on a tightrope, too. Should we then practice walking on a tightrope, setting up palms, or throwing our arms about statues? Of course, not. [Here, Epictetus seems to be mocking the Cynic's practice attributed to Diogenes of hugging statues naked in cold weather. Setting up palms could refer to climbing up a pole with only hands and feet.] Not everything difficult or dangerous is suitable for training, but only that which helps us achieve what we set out to achieve.

"What have we set ourselves to achieve?"

"To have our desires and aversions free from hindrance."

"What does that mean?"

"We should not fail to get what we desire or fall into what we would like to avoid. It is to this end our training should be directed. Without great and constant training, it is not possible to ensure that our desires will always be fulfilled, or we won't ever fall into what we would like to avoid."

You should know if you direct your training towards external things that lie outside your ability to choose, your desire will not be fulfilled, and you will not be able to avoid the things you would like to avoid.

Develop contrary habits to counter current habits

Habit is a powerful force. Because we have made it a habit of exercising our desires and aversions towards externals only, we must now oppose that habit with another, contrary, habit. Where impressions are most likely to mislead us, there we must apply our training to counter the risk.

First area of training:
Dealing with desires and aversions

"I'm inclined to pleasure."

"For the sake of training, move to the opposite direction more than you normally would."

"I have an aversion to suffering."

"Train yourself so your aversion to things of this nature is withdrawn."

"So, who is this person under training?"

"One who practises not exercising all her desires, and practises directing her aversion only in relation to things over which she has choice, practising particularly hard when things are highly challenging. So different people will have to practise hardest regarding different things. What purpose can it serve here – to set up a palm, to carry around a leather tent, and mortar and pestle?" [Cynics lived austerely and carried only a small number of items. Here, once again, Epictetus seems to be mocking their lifestyle.]

"I'm irritable."

"Train yourself to put up with abuse with patience. If you are insulted don't get angry."

Then you will progress so much that even if someone hits you, you can say to yourself, "Imagine that! You're hugging a statue."

Keep away from temptations when you begin training

Next, train yourself to use wine with discretion. Don't train to drink more – there are some so foolish as to train even for that – but to be able to keep away: first of all from wine, then from a pretty girl, or a sweet cake. Then, sometime in the future, you will venture into lists to test if you are still carried away by impressions as much as you once did. But when you start, keep well away from things that are stronger than you. A contest between a pretty girl and a budding philosopher is an unequal one. As the saying goes, "pot and stone don't belong to-gether."

Second area of training: Dealing with impulse to act or not to act

After your desire and your aversion, the next topic has to do with your choice or refusal – impulse to act or not to act. Here your aim is to make your impulse to act or not to act obedient to reason; not to exercise your choice at the wrong time or the in the wrong place, or wrongly in any other way.

Third area of training: Dealing with Assent

The third area of study is concerned with assent and with what is plausible and attractive. Just as Socrates used to say that we shouldn't live an unexamined life, so we shouldn't accept an unexamined impression but say, "Wait, let me see who you are and where you come from. Show me some identification. Do you have the identification from nature which every impression must carry, if it is to be accepted?"

Useful training should be directed inwards

All training applied to exercising the body may also be usefully applied to desires and aversions. But if they are directed towards showing off, it is a sign that you have turned to externals, hunting for some other victim and are seeking for an audience to applaud you, "What a great person!"

Thus, [the philosopher] Apollonius was right when he used to say, "If you want to train for your own sake, then, when you are thirsty in hot weather, take sip of cold water into your mouth and then spit it out. Don't tell anyone about it."

Think about this

Since habit is a powerful influence ... we must set a contrary habit to set this habit ... we must set our training as a counteracting force. Discourses III.12.6. Epictetus [WO]

DISCOURSE 13

Train to be Comfortable with Yourself

Key ideas of this discourse

1. *A desolate person is someone who is helpless, whether he is alone or with other people.*
2. *We should prepare ourselves to be self-sufficient and be able to live with ourselves.*
3. *Our rulers may guarantee safety against external dangers but not against internal turmoil. Only philosophy can guarantee internal peace and tranquillity. Once you see this, you will not be desolate anymore.*
4. *Train yourself to face hardships and help others by being an example to them.*

Being desolate is not the same as being alone

A desolate person is someone who is deprived of help. You are not desolate just because you are alone. Neither are you secure from desolation because you are in a

73

crowd. When, therefore we lose a son, a brother, or a friend whom we have relied upon, we say we have been left desolate, even if we live in a big city, where we constantly run into crowds, share our house with many people, and sometimes even have servants and assistants. The general meaning of desolation is that a person is helpless and exposed to those who wish him harm. That's why when we travel we call ourselves desolate – we are exposed to thieves. It is not just the sight of a person that relieves desolation, it is the sight of someone who can be trusted, who is honest and helpful.

If being alone is enough to make someone desolate, even God himself is desolate at the time of conflagration of the universe. [Ancient Stoics believed that the universe is periodically consumed and is reborn in fire.] He would lament to himself, "I don't have a wife or daughters. Neither do I have a brother, son, grandson or any other relative." There are some who say that he really acts this way when he finds himself alone at the conflagration of the universe. They say this because they cannot imagine how a person can live on their own, based on the natural principle that human beings are also social beings, are fond of each other, and enjoy associating with others.

We should prepare ourselves to be self-sufficient and be able to live with ourselves

Nevertheless, we should prepare ourselves to be self-sufficient and be able to live with ourselves. Even God lives with himself, converses with himself, thinks about the rules by which he governs the universe, and thinks thoughts that are worthy of him. Shouldn't we also be able to converse with ourselves, be self-sufficient, and know how to occupy ourselves? We should reflect on the divine governing order in our relationship to other things. We should consider how we used to respond to events and how we respond to them now, what things still bother us, and how to fix or remove them. If any of these need perfecting, we must perfect them in accordance with reason.

Governments cannot guarantee tranquillity, but philosophy can

The government seems to provide us with peaceful conditions. There are no wars, no battles, no large scale gang attacks, no robbery, safety when we travel or sail from dawn to dusk. But can the government promise us freedom from fever, from shipwreck, from fire, from earthquake, from lightning? No, not even from love. From grief? From envy? No, absolutely not.

But our philosophy principles promise to provide us with peace even from all these things. What do they say?

"If you heed me, wherever you may be, whatever you may be doing, you will feel no pain, no anger, no compulsion, no hindrance, but you'll pass your lives in tranquillity and in freedom from every disturbance."

When a person has this kind of peace granted to them – not by the government, how can it? – but by God through the voice of reason, isn't he content when he is alone as he thinks and considers this: "Now nothing bad can happen to me; there can be no robbers, no earthquake, and everything is peaceful and tranquil. Every road city, fellow-traveller, neighbour, and associate is harmless. The person who is responsible for food and clothing provides them to me. Another has given me senses and preconceptions. When he stops providing the necessities, he throws open the door and says, 'Go!'"

"Where to?"

"To nothing fearful. Only to that place from which you came. A place that is friendly and akin to you, akin to the elements. Whatever in you was of fire will return to fire; air to air, and water to water. There is no underworld or evil spirits. Everything is filled with gods and divine spirits." [Stoics did not accept the traditional beliefs about the afterlife and underworld. They thought the universe is full of divine spirit and providence.]

If you reflect on this and look upon the sea, moon, and stars and enjoy the earth and sea, you will not be desolate or helpless.

"What if someone attacks me when I'm alone and murders me?"

"They can't murder you, you fool, only your poor body."

Learn from the simplicity of children

What desolation is left then? What helplessness? Why do we make ourselves worse than little children? What do they do when left alone? They gather up pieces of pottery and dirt and build something out of them. They tear it down and build something else. They are never short of amusement.

If you all sail away, should I sit down and cry because I am left alone and desolate? Don't I have my pottery and dirt? When children act that way, they do so in their simplicity; are we to act unhappy through our wisdom?

[*Here there is an abrupt transition of subject matter. It is possible that the rest of the Discourse should belong somewhere else.*]

Training to cope with adverse conditions

Any great power is dangerous to the beginner. Therefore, we should bear such things according to our capacity, and in accordance with nature... [*There seems to be a gap in text here.*] but not for a consumptive.

Practice one time living like someone who is ill, so you can live like a healthy person in another. Take no food, just drink water.

Abstain from every desire at one time to be able to exercise your desires in a reasonable way at a later time. If you do so in a reasonable way, when you have some good in you, your desires will be good as well.

How to help others

But no, you want to live as a wise man right now and bring benefit to others. What kind of benefit? Were you able to help yourself? And yet you want to help others progress. Have you made progress yourself? Do you want to help them? Then show them by your own example the kind of person philosophy produces. Stop talking nonsense.

- Bring benefit to those who eat with you, by the way in which you eat.
- Bring benefit to those who drink with you, by the way in which you drink.
- Help them by yielding to them, by giving way to them, and not showering them with your spittle!

Think about this

A person is not desolate merely because he is alone, any more than he is secure from desolation because he is in a crowd. Discourses III.13.1. Epictetus [RH]

Get Rid of
Conceit and Diffidence

Key ideas of this discourse

1. *Ascetic practices should bring you some benefit. Otherwise, they are ridiculous.*
2. *Even if your practice brings you some benefit, don't go telling everyone. Not everyone will like it.*
3. *Get rid of conceit and diffidence.*
4. *Prove yourself superior in qualities that are uniquely human. Don't try to take credit for qualities that don't truly belong to you.*

Asceticism is ridiculous
if you practice for the sake of practicing it

Bad choral singers cannot sing on their own, but only with many others. Likewise, some people cannot walk on their own. If you are anyone at all, walk on your own, talk to yourself, and do not hide yourself in the chorus. Put

up with being laughed at sometimes. Look around you
and shake yourself up to learn who you are.

If it benefits you, don't broadcast it

When someone adopts an ascetic practice such as drinking water only, he grabs every opportunity to tell everyone who comes across

"I drink nothing but water."

"Why, do you drink only water merely for the sake of
drinking it? Man, if it is beneficial to you, drink it. If not,
you are being ridiculous. If drinking only water benefits
you, don't talk about it to those irritated by it. Why do
you do it? Aren't these the very people you are trying to
please?"

Some actions are performed for their own sake; others as demanded by circumstances, as a matter of good
management, to accommodate others, or as a part of our
life plan.

Get rid of conceit and diffidence

We should get rid of two things: conceit and diffidence.

• *Conceit* is assuming that there is nothing more
you can need.
• *Diffidence* is assuming that it is impossible to find
serenity under adverse conditions.

You can get rid of conceit through cross-examination,
like Socrates did. [*There is a gap in text here.*] This is not
impossible but it is something you must examine and

investigate. Such an investigation will not harm you. In fact, the practice of philosophy is virtually that – investigating how it is possible to exercise one's desires and aversions without hindrance.

Excel in qualities that are uniquely human

"I'm better than you. My father is of consular rank," says one.

"I've been a prestigious official and you haven't," [says another.]

If you are a horse, would you say, "I have plenty of barley and fodder," or, "I have lovely trappings"?

What if you spoke that way and I say, "Be that as it may. Let's run a race."

Is there nothing in the human activity comparable to a race in horses, which will decide who is better or who is worse? Is there no such thing as honour, or faithfulness, or justice? Prove yourself superior in these so you may be a better human being. But if you tell me that you have a powerful kick, I will answer, "You are proud of a donkey's quality."

Think about this

Isn't there such a thing as reverence, faith, justice? Prove yourself superior in these points, in order to be superior as a human being. Discourses III.14.13. Epictetus [WO]

Approach Everything Carefully

Key ideas of this discourse

1. In everything you do, consider what comes before and what comes after and only then act.
2. Not everyone is suited to do everything. Different people are made for different things.
3. Decide what you want to do and do it fully.
4. Becoming a philosopher requires that one should be very disciplined. If you want to become a philosopher, make sure you are willing to pay the price.

Before undertaking anything, consider what is involved

In everything you do, consider what comes before and what comes after and then only act. Otherwise, you will start eagerly at first, but since you have not given any thought to what might follow, you will give it up in a shameful manner.

"I want to win at the Olympics."

Yes, but consider what comes first and what comes after and then, if it is to your advantage, set to work. You must accept the discipline, submit to the diet, stay away from pastries, train as you are ordered at the appointed time, in heat or cold. You must not drink cold water or wine as you like. In short, you should hand yourself to your trainer as you would to a doctor. Then, when the time for the contest arrives you have to compete in digging [the practice of covering yourself with mud before a wrestling match], sometimes dislocate your wrist, sprain your ankle, and swallow quantities of sand and get whipped. And then, get defeated sometimes – after all that! Reflect on these things. Then, if you still want to become an athlete, go for it.

Otherwise, know that you are behaving like children who sometimes play wrestlers, sometimes gladiators, sometimes blow a trumpet, and then play act whatever they have seen and admired. Likewise, you're an athlete sometimes, gladiator sometimes; now a philosopher, and then an orator; but nothing wholeheartedly. Like an ape, you imitate whatever you see. One thing after another catches your fancy, but it stops pleasing you, once you become familiar with it. You have never started on anything with enough consideration, have never examined the entire thing carefully and systematically, but have always approached things randomly and half-heartedly.

STOIC TRAINING • 85

Different people are made for different things

Thus, some people, when they see and hear someone who speaks like [the Stoic philosopher] Euphrates – and yet, who can speak like him? – want to be philosophers themselves too. But first consider what you are taking on, then your own nature, and what you can endure. If you want to be a wrestler, you will have to look to your shoulders, your back, and your thighs. For different people are made for different things.

Becoming a philosopher requires discipline

Do you think you can act the way you do and yet become a philosopher? That you can eat and drink like you do now, and be angry and irritable? You must stay up at night, you must work hard, overcome certain desires, abandon your people, be scorned by a slave, laughed at by those who meet you; come off worse than others in everything: in office, in honour, and in the courts. When you have considered all these drawbacks carefully, if you still think it fit, then approach philosophy. Be willing to give up all of this in exchange for serenity, freedom, and peace of mind.

Otherwise don't come near. Don't behave like a child – now a philosopher, then a tax collector, then an orator, and then a procurator of Caesar. These things don't go together. You must be one person – good or bad. You must cultivate either your ruling faculty or external things. In short, you must assume either the role of philosopher or of a lay person.

[*The following exchange seems unconnected to the rest of the discourse.*]

When [the emperor] Galba was murdered, someone asked [Musonius] Rufus:

"So is the universe governed by providence *now*?"

Rufus replied:

"Have I ever, even casually, used the example of Galba to show that the universe is governed by providence?"

Think about this

In each action that you undertake, consider what comes before and what follows after, and only then proceed to the action itself. Discourses III.15.1. Epictetus [RH]

Train on Your Principles Before Venturing Out

Key ideas of this discourse

1. *Either you influence your friends, or they influence you.*
2. *The stronger will influence the weaker. If those who talk nonsense have stronger convictions, they will influence you.*
3. *Therefore, until you train yourself strongly in your principles, be careful who you associate yourself with.*

Either you influence others or others influence you

If you associate with others on a regular basis – for small talk, for parties, or for friendship – you will necessarily grow up to be like them, unless you get them to be like you. If you place a dead coal by a live one, either the live coal will set fire to the dead one or the dead coal will put out the live one. Since the stakes are high, you should be careful about socializing with lay people. Remember, it is impossible to rub against someone covered with dirt and avoid getting dirty yourself. What will you do if they talk about gladiators, horses, and sport heroes? Or worse, gossip about others – "So-and-so is good, and so-and-so is bad; this is well done and that's done poorly"? Or if they taunt you, ridicule you, or even be of an ill-nature?

If you are not strong, it is others who will influence you

Do any of you have the ability of the musician who can pick up an instrument, identify right away which strings are out of tune, and so bring the whole instrument into tune? Or the ability of Socrates, who could win over the company to his side in every conversation? How could you? Most likely, you are going to adopt their mentality.

Why are they stronger than you? Because they talk their nonsense with conviction while your fine points come out of your lips. Your talk has no vigour, no life. It will turn people's stomachs to hear you go on and on about your miserable "virtue." So, they get the better of you. Conviction is all-powerful and irresistible. So, until these fine points take firm root in you and you can start relying on them safely, I advise you to be careful in associating with such people. Otherwise, whatever you write down here will melt away like wax in the sun. So long as your opinions are merely like wax, keep well out of the sun.

Fix your principles and put them into practice

Philosophers even advise us to leave our country because bad habits pull us back and make it harder for us to develop new ones. Besides, we can't stand running into people who say, "Oh, look, this so-and-so has turned into a philosopher!" It is for such reasons doctors send their most chronic patients to a different place and a different climate. And rightly so.

Adopt new habits yourself. Fix your principles and put them into practice.

Keep the right company until your principles take firm roots

No. Instead you go from here to the theatre, to the gladiators, to the circus. Back here again, back there again. And you remain the same all the time. No sign of better habits, no attention to yourself. You don't watch yourself carefully and ask:

"How do I deal with impressions that come my way? In accordance with nature or against it? Do I respond to them as I should, or don't I? Do I tell external things that they are nothing to me?"

If you are not at this stage [of understanding], and yet hope to become somebody, give up your old habits and stay away from lay people.

Think about this

Keep well out of the sun, then, as long as your principles are as pliant as wax. Discourses III.16.10. Epictetus [RD]

Train Yourself to See Things as They Are

Key ideas of this discourse

1. *Everything that happens, happens in accordance with reason. People who are wealthier pay a price for being wealthy. So, it is reasonable that they have what they have.*
2. *Don't add judgments to events and make them worse..*

People have what they have because they paid the price

Whenever you find fault with providence, reflect on it. You will then realize that what happened is reasonable.

"True. But the dishonest person is better off."

"In what? In money? Yes, in that regard he is better off, because he flatters people, he is shameless, and lies awake at night. Nothing surprising there. But look to see if he is better than you in being trustworthy and honest?

You will not find it to be so. Where you are superior to him, there you are better than him."

Someone was upset because he was envious of the wealth of another. [Epictetus] asked him

"Will you be willing to sleep with senator so-and-so?"

"God forbid such a day should ever come!"

"Then why are you angry with the wealthy man [who slept with the senator to gain his wealth]? He paid for it. How can you think that he is fortunate when he got what he wanted using means which you detest? What harm does providence do in giving better things to better people? Isn't it better to be honourable than be rich?"

"You are right."

"Then why are you upset, if you have things of greater worth? Always remember and keep this thought at hand: It is a law of nature that the superior person has the advantage over the inferior person in respect to the superiority. You will never ever have any reason to be upset."

Don't add your judgment to events

"But my wife behaves badly towards me."

"Well, if someone asks what's the matter, say, 'My wife behaves badly to me.'"

"Nothing more?"

"No."

"My father doesn't give me anything."

[*There is a gap in text here.*]

"Do you have to add in your mind the judgment that it is bad (which is untrue)?

For this reason, it is not poverty we should reject, but the judgment we hold about it. Then we will be at peace.

Think about this

It is not poverty we should reject, but our judgement regarding it, and then we shall be at peace. Discourses III.17.9. Epictetus [CG/RH]

Nothing External Can Harm You

Key ideas of this discourse

1. *News is concerned with external things. So, it cannot harm you.*
2. *You should be concerned only about things over which you have real choice.*
3. *The way others behave is up to them. It is no concern of yours*

Disturbing news cannot affect you

Whenever you receive any disturbing news, keep this thought ready at hand: The news cannot affect anything that is of your choice. Who can bring the news saying that you are mistaken in your assumption or your desires are inappropriate? No one.

"But someone can bring the news that so-and-so has died."

"What is it to you?"

"So-and-so is speaking badly of me."

"What is it to you?"

"My father is hatching some scheme or other."

"Against what? Against your choice? How could he? Well, against your poor body or property. You are safe then. It's not against you."

"But the judge just found me guilty of impiety."

"Didn't the judges do the same in the case of Socrates? Is the judgment any business of yours? No. Then why worry about it?"

Others' actions cannot harm you

Your father has to do some things. If he doesn't do them, he will lose his character as a father, a man who loves his children and is gentle towards them. Do not try to make him lose something more because of that.

It is never the case that one person does something wrong and someone else suffers harm. Your job is to defend yourself strongly, respectfully, and without anger. Otherwise, you will lose your character as a son, respected and noble-minded.

Is the judge free from danger? No, he is exposed to an equal risk as well. Why are you then afraid of his decision? What does someone's evil have to do with you?

You should only concern yourself with your choices

Making a bad defence will be your own evil. You should guard only against that. But whether you are condemned or acquitted is someone else's business. It is also that person's evil.

"So-and-so is threatening me."

"You? No."

"She is blaming me."

"It is for her to look to how she manages her own business."

"He is going to condemn me unjustly."

"Poor wretch!"

Think about this

News never relates to anything that lies within your sphere of choice. Discourses III.18.1. [RD]

Your Judgment Is the Sole Cause of Your Distress

Key ideas of this discourse

1. *Only your choices can cause you distress.*
2. *We tend be distressed because we have been following the wrong course of action since our childhood.*
3. *We have been brought up from the beginning to believe that external things cause us distress. So, we behave like children.*

Only your choices can cause you distress

The first difference between a philosopher and a layperson is this: The layperson says, "Oh, how I suffer because of my child, because of my brother, because of my father," whereas the philosopher, if compelled, says, "Oh, how I suffer," thinks about it and adds, "because of myself."

Choice cannot be hindered or hurt by anything out-side your area of choice, only by choice itself. So, when-ever you go astray, if you are so inclined, blame yourself for it. And if you remember that nothing except your own judgment can cause you to become disturbed or confused, then I swear to you by all the gods that we've made progress.

We have been following the wrong course

But, in fact, we have been following a different course from the beginning, even when we were children, If we ever bumped into something, our nurse, instead of telling us off, would hit the stone. Why? What has the stone done? Should it have moved out of your way because you we were being foolish?

Again, if we couldn't find anything to eat after our bath, our attendant didn't try to moderate our appetite but punished the cook instead. Why, did we appoint you attendant of the cook? No, but of the child. It is she whom you are to correct and improve.

The result? Even when we are all grown up, we resem-ble children. After all, it is being a child to be unculti-vated in matters of culture, unschooled in matters of literature, and uneducated in matters relating to the art of living.

Think about this

Nothing except our own judgement is capable of causing us to become disturbed and confused. Discourses III.19.3. Epictetus [RD]

Train to Spot an Advantage in Every Circumstance

Key ideas of this discourse

1. *Good and bad come from us, not from external events.*
2. *You can derive benefit from any external event – even sickness and death.*
3. *If someone is "bad", he is bad for himself, not to you. Your good and bad come from the choices you make.*

Good and bad come from ourselves, not from external events

Regarding intellectual impressions, almost everyone agrees that the good and bad come from ourselves, not from things external to us. No one says that the statement, "It's day," is good or the statement, "It's night," is bad. Nor does anyone say, "Three is equal to four," the greatest evil.

"What do they say, then?"

"Knowledge is good and error is bad. Even in what is false, good can arise, namely, the knowledge is indeed false. The same should be true in life as well. Is health a good and illness an evil?"

"No."

"What then? Health is good when put to good use and bad when put to bad use."

"So, it is possible to benefit even from sickness?"

"For heaven's sake, is it not possible to benefit even from death? And from lameness? Isn't it so? Was it only a small benefit that Menoeceus [who gave up his life to save the city of Thebes] gained when he died?"

"May the person who talks like that gain the same sort of benefit as he did!

There is benefit even in sickness and death

"Listen, didn't he preserve his character as a patriot, and as one who was magnanimous, faithful, and noble-spirited? Had he survived, wouldn't he have lost all those qualities and acquired the opposite qualities? Wouldn't his character be that of someone who is cowardly, mean-spirited, a hater of his country, and lover his own life? Well now, do you think he gained only a small benefit from his death? No?

Well, how about the father of Admetus [who refused to die in spite of being very old himself in order to save the life of his son]? Did he gain any advantage by refusing

STOIC TRAINING • 105

to die, in a wretched and miserable fashion? And later, did he not die anyway?"

You must stop, I command you by the gods, admiring material things, stop making yourself a slave, first of things and then, on account of these things, to people who are able to get them for you or take them away from you.

"Is it possible, then, to benefit from these things?"

"Yes, from everything."

"Even from someone who insults me?"

"What advantage does a wrestler get from his sparring partner? The greatest. Well, the person who insults you is your sparring partner. He trains you in patience, in being free of anger, and in gentleness."

You disagree. Yet the man who grips your neck and gets your hips and shoulders in shape brings you benefit. The wrestling coach does well in telling you, "Raise the weight with both hands." And the heavier the weight, the more good it does you. Yet you say that one who trains you in being free of anger brings you no benefit. It is simply that you don't know how to draw benefit from other people.

If someone is "bad," he is bad for himself, not to you

Your neighbour is bad? Bad to himself, but good to you.

This is the magic wand of Hermes [son of Zeus]: As the saying goes, "Touch what you like, it will turn into gold." For me, bring me anything and I'll turn it into something good. Bring sickness, death, poverty, abuse, or even a trial for your own life. All these, under the touch of the wand of Hermes, will become a source of benefit.

"What about death?"

"What else but make it to your glory or an opportunity for you to show in action what kind of a person it is who follows the will of nature."

"What about disease?"

"I'll show its nature, I will get the better of it and remain steadfast and serene. I will neither flatter my doctor nor pray for my death. What more do you want? Whatever you give me, I will turn it into something blessed and a source of happiness; something imposing and admirable."

But not you. You say, "Watch out. Don't get sick. It's bad." It's like saying "Watch out. Don't get the impression that three equals four. It's bad. In what way is it bad, my friend? If I get the right idea about it, how can it harm me anymore? Will it not even be beneficial to me? If I form the right idea about poverty, or disease, or not holding office, isn't that enough for me? Will it not help me? How then do you expect me to seek for good any longer in external things?"

But what is the reality? You accept these ideas as far as the door but no one takes them home with them. All at once you are at war with your servants, your neighbours and those who laugh at you. Thank you [Epictetus' critic] Lesbius, for proving every day that I know nothing!

Think about this

Even in regard to what is false, there arises a good. Discourses III.20.3. Epictetus [WO]

Don't Imitate Others Blindly

Key ideas of this discourse

1. To be an expert you should first digest what you have learned.
2. Don't imitate the actions of others without understanding the foundations.
3. Until you have digested what you have learned and understood fully what is involved, act with modesty and don't imitate people who know much better than you.

Show your mastery through results

People who have learned principles in theory want to vomit them up immediately, just as those with weak stomachs throw up their food. Digest the principles first, and you won't vomit them up this way. Otherwise they just turn into vomit – foul food, unfit to eat. But, after you have digested them, show a change in your ruling centre that is due to those principles, just as athletes can show their shoulders because of their training and diet, or as master artists can show the results of their learning. A builder doesn't come up and say, "Listen to my discourse on the art of building," but gets a contract and builds a house. He thereby shows he has mastered the art of building. You should do likewise. Eat like a human being, drink like a human being, dress, marry, become a parent, assume your social responsibilities, put up with abuses; put up with an inconsiderate brother, a father, a son, neighbour, and fellow-traveller. Show these things so we can see that you really have learned something from philosophers.

But, no. You say, "Come and listen to me reading out my commentaries!" Go away. Find someone else to vomit over.

"Yes, but I can explain Chrysippus' writings to you as no one else can; analyse his language and style with perfect clarity; and I will even add some sparkle of Antipater and Archedemus."

So, is it for this then that young people should leave their homelands and parents, to hear you interpret trivial phrases? Shouldn't they go back home as patient people, helpful to others, tranquil, with a mind at peace? Shouldn't they be furnished with all they need for their journey through life, so they can face up to everything that comes about and derive honour from it? But how can you pass on to them what you yourself don't have? Have you done anything else since the beginning than to spend all your time trying to solve syllogisms, equivocal arguments, and those developed through questioning?

Don't imitate the actions of others.
Understand what's involved

"But so-and-so lectures. Why shouldn't I do the same?"

"It's not something you can do at random and without proper thought, idiot. One must be of the right age, follow a certain way of life, and have the guidance of gods. You don't agree. Yet no one sails from a harbour without first offering the gods a sacrifice and praying for their help. No one sows the fields casually but only after praying for help from Demeter [the goddess of agriculture]."

So, can anyone start on such important work as this without the help of gods? Will those who approach gods meet with good fortune? What are you doing, other than profaning the Mysteries and declaring,

"Look, just as there is a shrine there, there's one here too; there is a priest there, I will get one here too; there is a state official there, I will appoint one here too; there are torches there, there will be torches here too."

Both can speak the same words. So, what's the difference between what happens there and what happens here? Are you saying there is no difference, you most impious man? Do these actions bring you the same benefits if they are carried out in the wrong place and at the wrong time? Shouldn't you approach with sacrifices and prayers? Don't they require that you purify yourself first? And that your mind hold the thought that you are coming here to participate in sacred rites that are of ancient antiquity? Is this any way to benefit from Mysteries? Is this any way to appreciate that all these things were established by people of earlier generations for our education and the betterment of our lives?

When you imitate without understanding, you are trivializing

As far as you are concerned, you are divulging it to everyone. You are spoofing them and placing them outside their proper time and place, without sacrifices, without purification. You don't wear the costume that the priest should wear; you don't have the right hair or headband. You don't have the right voice, you are not of the right age, you have not kept yourself pure like the other person has, but you have been satisfied just to steal the words he utters and recite them. Do you think words are sacred in themselves?

Approach with caution and respect

You need to approach this very differently. This is a great mission, a serious mystery and is not granted to anyone who comes along. Even being wise may not be enough to take care of the young. You should have a special aptitude and inclination and, by God, a particular physique. You need a calling from God to fulfil this function, just as Socrates was called to fulfil the function of correcting the errors of others, as Diogenes was called to fulfil the function of regally reprimanding them, and as Zeno was called to fulfil the function of teaching and establishing the principles of philosophy.

Instead, you want to start practicing as a doctor, having nothing more than your medicines. You neither know nor have taken the time to learn when and how you should apply them. "Look at him. He has those eye salves. I have just the same!" Do you know how to use them? Do you have any idea when and how they will do any good? And to whom?

Be aware of your limitations

Why, then, are you putting in danger matters of the highest importance? Why are you careless? Leave it to those who can do it and do it well. Don't bring disgrace to philosophy by your actions like many others do. If philosophical principles interest you, sit down and work on them yourself. But don't say that you are a philosopher and don't let anyone else say that you are one. Say instead, "He is mistaken. My desires are not different from what they were before, nor are they directed towards other things. I don't assent to other things than what I used to. And I am not able to interpret impressions any better." If you think correctly, this is what you must think and say to yourself. Otherwise, act recklessly: do what you are doing. That's what you are suited for.

Think about this

You open up shop as a doctor with no other equipment than your medicines: as to when or how you should apply them, that you neither know nor have ever bothered to learn.

"Look, that man has those eye salves and I have just the same." Do you have the ability, then, to make proper use of *them?* Discourse III.21.21. Epictetus [RH]

Training to Be a Philosopher

Key ideas of this discourse

[In this discourse, Epictetus presents an idealized version of a philosopher, in the context of a student expressing an interest in Cynicism, which provided inspiration for Stoicism. Although the descriptions refer to a Cynic philosopher, it would apply equally to a Stoic philosopher.]

1. *Don't imitate the actions of others without understanding why.*
2. *To be an expert, you should first digest what you have learned.*
3. *Until you have digested what you have learned and understood fully what is involved, act with modesty and don't imitate people who know much better than you.*
4. *A philosopher would care for others and take care of them. He knows that good and bad come out of his choices. His desires are always fulfilled, and he is never*

faced with anything that he is averse to. He is charming, witty, and physically healthy. But he surrenders his body to others if necessary. He may not marry and bring up children but contributes to society in other ways.

5. *A life like that needs a lot of training. If you want to become a philosopher, review your resources and make sure you are up to it.*

Show your mastery through results

One of his students who was attracted to Cynicism asked Epictetus,

"Who is qualified to be a Cynic?"

"Let us examine the idea at length," said Epictetus.

But first let me tell you this much. If someone attempts to understand this great topic while not believing in God or hating him, it is nothing but disgraceful behaviour in front of the public. In a well-managed house, not anyone can declare, "I should be running this place." If you do, the master of the house will see you giving orders and you will be dragged away and thrown out. It is so with this world, too. For here is a master of the house who orders everything. He says,

- "You are the sun. Go around and make the year and seasons. Make the fruits and nourish them. Stir the winds and make them calm. Warm people's bodies. Go, travel around, and manage things from the greatest to the least."

- "You are cow. When a lion appears, run away. If you don't, you'll suffer."

- "You are a bull. Step forward and fight the lion, because this is your business. It becomes you and you can do it.
- "You are capable of leading an army against Troy. Be Agamemnon."
- "You are capable of fighting against Hector in a single combat. Be Achilles."

But if [the inferior fighter] Thersites had come forward to claim the command, he wouldn't have got it. If he had, he would have disgraced himself in front of several witnesses.

Don't get carried away by superficial symbols

Likewise, you should think about the matter carefully: it's not the way it looks. You say,

"I wear a coarse cloak now and I will wear it then. I sleep on a hard bed now and I will be on one then. In addition, now and then, I will take a little bag and a staff and beg from the people I meet, and abuse them. If I see anyone dressing his hair or walking about in purple, I will rebuke them."

If you imagine this is what it takes to be a Cynic, keep well away. Don't come near it. It's not at all for you. But if you imagine it as it really is and do not consider yourself unfit for it, consider what a great thing you undertake.

You need to change the way you think

First, about yourself. You must not, in any in instance, behave the way you do now. You must accuse neither God nor others. You must completely get rid of desire, and must be averse only to those things that are your choices. You should not give in to anger, resentment, envy, or pity. A girl or a boy should not look pretty or handsome to you, nor must you love reputation or be pleased by a cake. You should know that, when people do things of this nature, they are protected by walls, houses, and darkness. They have much to conceal. A man shuts the doors, stations someone outside his bedroom and says, "If someone comes calling say, 'He's out, he is busy.'"

Instead of all this, a Cynic uses only his honour as his protection. If he doesn't, he will be indecent when he is naked under the open sky. Honour is his house, his door, his doorkeeper, and his darkness. He must not wish to hide anything he does. If he does, he is gone, he has lost his character of a Cynic, of a free and outdoor character. He has begun to fear some external thing and has a need to hide something. Nor does he can he hide when he wants to. Where will he hide and how? If, by any chance, this public teacher gets caught, what must this instructor suffer? Can someone who is afraid of all this still have the confidence to supervise others? No. It is not practical, and it is not possible.

So, in the first place, you must make your ruling faculty pure and develop a corresponding life style.

"Just as the material for a carpenter is wood, and the material for a shoemaker is leather, the material I need to work on from now on is my own mind. The body or its parts are nothing to me. Death? Let death come whenever it chooses, either to the whole body or a part. 'Fly,' you say. And to where? Can you banish me from this universe? You cannot. But, wherever I go, there will be sun, there will be moon, there will be stars, dreams, prophesies, and conversation with gods."

Even this preparation is not sufficient for a true Cynic. He must know that he has been sent by God to be a messenger to people about good and bad things. To show them that they have wandered and are looking for the nature of good and bad in the wrong places, rather than where it really is.

Understand where good and bad lie

After the battle of Chaeroneia, Diogenes was brought to Philip. A Cynic is indeed a spy – a spy of what is good and what is bad. It is his duty to examine carefully and report accurately thus: not to be struck with terror because there are no enemies, not to be confused in any other way by impressions. If necessary, it is his duty then to climb on to the tragic stage and, like Socrates, say,

"Tell me, where are you going in such a hurry? What are you doing, miserable ones? You are wandering up and down like blind people. You have left the true road and are going into a cul-de-sac. You look for peace and happiness where they are not. If someone shows where they

are, you don't believe them. Why are you seeking it outside?"

- *In the body?* It's not there. If you doubt it, look at
[the contemporary gladiators and athletes] Myro
and Ophelius [who presumably came to a bad
end.]
- *In possessions?* It's not there. If you do not believe
me, look at Croesus [who was presumably mur-
dered]. Look at those who are now rich and see
how much they complain.
- *In power?* It's not there. If it is, people who hold
high offices must be happy; they are not."

Whom shall we believe in these matters? You who
view this from outside and are dazzled by appearances,
or the men themselves? What do they say? Hear them
when they groan, when they grieve, when they think that
they are worse off and at greater risk just because they
hold high offices.

- *In royal power?* It's not there. Otherwise Nero and
[the last king of Assyria] Sardanapalus would have
been happy. Not even Agamemnon, who was a
better man than them, was happy. When the rest
were snoring, what did he do?

"He pulled a hair from his head, roots and all."

What did he say?

*"I pace up and down. My spirit is troubled, and my heart
is pounding right out of my chest."* [*Iliad*, x.15, 91, 94-95.
RD]

Poor man, what is going badly for you? Your possessions? No. Your body? No. But you are rich in "God and

bronze." What is wrong with you then? Your problem is that you have neglected and ruined that faculty with which you feel desire and aversion, impulse to act or not to act.

"Neglected how?"

"By not learning the true nature of good to which it is born and of the nature of evil, or learning what belongs to it and what doesn't. When something that is not its own goes badly, it thinks, 'Poor me, the Greeks under attack.'"

"Too bad for your mind, the one thing you have neglected by not taking care of it.

"Trojans will kill us."

"And, if they don't kill you, won't you die anyway?"

"Yes, but not all at once."

"What difference does it make? If death is wrong, it is wrong whether it is singly or together. After all, death means nothing more than the separation of body and soul. If the Greeks die, do they close the door behind them? Isn't it in your power to die?"

"It is."

"Why complain then while you are a king and hold the sceptre of Zeus? A king cannot become unfortunate any more than a god can. So, what does that make you? A shepherd, and rightly so. You whine, like shepherds do, when a wolf snatches one of their sheep. And the people you rule over too – they are mere sheep. Anyway, why did you come? Was your desire in any danger? Or your choice, impulse to act, or aversion?"

"No, my sister-in-law was abducted."

"Isn't it a blessing to be rid of an adulterous wife?"

"Should we let the Trojans insult us, then?"

"What are the Trojans? Are they wise or foolish? If wise, why fight with them? If foolish, what does it matter what they think?

"If these things are not important, where does our good lie? Tell us, oh our Great Messenger and spy!"

"It's not where you think it is, or where you look for it. Otherwise, you would have found that it is within you. You would not be wandering looking for it outside of yourself. You would not seek after what is not your own as though it is. Direct your thoughts towards yourself. Examine your preconceived ideas. What do you think good is?"

"Good is serenity, happiness, and freedom."

"Excellent. Don't you think that it is naturally great, priceless, and cannot be harmed? Where are you going to find them then? In something free or in something enslaved?"

"In the free."

"Is your body free or enslaved?

"I don't know."

"Don't you think that your body is a slave to fever, gout, eye-disease and dysentery, not to mention tyrants, fire, and steel? In fact, everything stronger than itself?"

"Yes, it is."

"Then, how can the body, or any of its parts, be free? Or be great or priceless? In essence, it is lifeless, mere mud and dust. Do you have anything that is free?"

"I don't think I do."

"Well, can anyone force you to agree to what appears to you to be wrong?"

"No."

"Can anyone force you to deny to what is plainly true?"

"No."

"So, you do have something in you that, by nature, is free. Now, can you desire or avoid, choose or refuse, plan or anticipate, until you have first formed an impression of what is proper or improper?"

"No."

"So, here too, you have something free and independent. Why not try focussing on that and look after that, you poor devil? This is where you should look for your good."

"But if someone has nothing – no clothes, no home or fireplace, no clean place, no one who would assist, no city – how is it possible for a person like that to be happy?"

"God has sent us someone like that to show that it is indeed possible. 'Look at me. I have no country, no home, no possessions, and no servants. I sleep on the ground. I don't have a wife or children or fine residence, just earth and sky and one sorry cloak. And what do I lack? Am I not without sorrow, without fear? Am I not free? Have you even seen me fail to get what I want or get what I try to avoid? Have I ever blamed God or another human being? Have I ever yelled at anyone? Have you ever seen me with a sad face? How do I treat people whom you fear and stand in awe of? Do I not treat them as if they were slaves? As a matter of fact, whenever they see me, they treat me as their lord and master.' This is the language of a Cynic, this is his character and this is his personality."

Instead you think you can tell a Cynic by his satchel, his stick, and his jaws; by the way he wolfs down or stores away the food given to him, by the way he shouts abuses at passers-by or by his bare, broad shoulders. Do you see the way in which you propose to take this great endeavour on? Look in the mirror. Look at your shoulders, check out your back and thighs. You are about to enrol yourself in the Olympics, not in some poor, second-rate competition. If you lose at the Olympics, you can't just leave. You are first disgraced in front of the whole world, not just people from your city or country. A casual contestant who thinks he can leave whenever he likes will be crushed, but not before he suffers thirst and heat and swallows a handful of sand.

Being a Cynic is not easy

So, think more carefully, know your limits, don't go forward without the help of God. If he advises you, you will be a great man, but you will also suffer a great many blows. This is a part of a Cynic's destiny: he must be beaten like a donkey and, when he is beaten, must love those who beat him as though they were his father or brother.

No, that's not how you would react. If someone beats you, you'd cry publicly: "O Caesar, why do I suffer like this when you have brought peace to the world? Take me to the proconsul [*governor and judge*] at once."

What is Caesar to a Cynic? What is the proconsul? What is anyone else except God who sent him here and whose mission he serves? He doesn't call upon anyone else. He is confident that, if he faces hardship, it is God who put him through it to train him. Heracles, when he was trained by Eurystheus, did not consider himself miserable but performed all labours required of him. Should we expect a Cynic, who argues that he takes orders from God who is his trainer, to hesitate or complain?

Listen what Diogenes said, when he had a fever, to those passing by. "Fools, where are you going in a hurry? You are going a long way to watch the battles or to watch the downfall of athletes in the Olympics. Don't you want to see the battle between a man and his illness?" He positively prides himself in facing difficult situations and thinks of himself as a worthy spectacle to those who pass by him. Such a man will not accuse the god who chose him and sent him here of treating him unfairly. What would he accuse God of? That he is so dignified? What would his charge be? That his virtue shines brightly?

What does Diogenes say about poverty, death, and pain? How does he compare his happiness with that of a Persian King? Or, rather, he thinks that there's no comparison. After all, where you find restlessness, grief, fear, disappointed desires, failed aversions, jealousy and envy, there happiness cannot enter. When your judgments are false, these passions will naturally follow.

You must be a Cynic
to be worthy of a Cynic's friendship

The same young man asked:

"If a Cynic got sick, should he agree to be taken care of by a friend, if invited?"

"Where will you find a friend of a Cynic? He would have to be another Cynic, just like you. He would have to 'share the sceptre and kingdom,' [The Cynic is presented here as the true king] and be a worthy minister [of God], if he is to be honoured with the friendship."

Thus, Diogenes was worthy of Antisthenes and Crates of Diogenes. Or, do you imagine that anyone who salutes a Cynic will be accepted as a friend worthy of being invited into his home? If that's what you think, you better start looking for a rubbish heap to shelter you from the North Wind when you get a fever, so you may not catch a chill. But it looks to me as though all you want to do is to get into someone's house and be well-fed for a while. You have no business trying to undertake so great a subject as Cynicism. The student asked:

"But, can a Cynic choose to marry and have children?"

"In a city of sages, it is quite possible that no one would live the life of a Cynic. For whose sake would he do it? But, supposing there is a Cynic there, then nothing would prevent him from marrying and having children. His wife and her father would be like him, his children would be brought up to be like him. But now everything is ordered as though for a battle. Isn't it necessary that a Cynic be free from distraction, dedicated to his sacred ministry, ready to walk around? If he is tied down to private obligations and mixed up in relationships that he cannot very well ignore, can he still maintain his character as a wise and good man? If he remains faithful to them, will it not destroy his nature as a messenger and spy carrying a divine message?"

He contributes to society by the way he lives and looks after others

Let me give you a few examples. He has some obligations to his father-in-law, some to the relatives of his wife, and some to his wife herself. From now on, whenever he has to be a provider for them or be a nurse for them when they are sick, he cannot carry out his calling [as a Cynic]. He has to have other things as well: a container for warm water for the bad; warm clothing for his wife when she has a child; plus oil, and a bed, and a cup. See how quickly they all add up! There will be so many other things that would fill his mind and distract him.

Let me ask you this. After all the above, where will the king, who devotes all his time for public good, be? Where is the king whose duty it is to watch over others who are married and have children, to supervise which one is treating their spouse well, which badly, who is fighting, which households are thriving, and which are not? The king is like a doctor. He goes around like a doctor who takes the pulse of her patients saying, "You have fever," "You have headache," "You have the gout," "You should fast," "You should eat," "You should not bathe," "You need an operation," and "You need to be cauterized."

How is someone burdened by private duties going to find time for this? Shouldn't he provide his children clothes and send them off to school with their notebooks and pens and make up a bed for them at night? They cannot be Cynics straight out of their mother's womb! If he fails to do all this, he might as well have exposed them at birth and kill them off that way [than by neglect].

Do you see to what level we have reduced a Cynic? How we are depriving him of his kingdom?

"But [the Cynic philosopher] Crates was married." "Yes, but that was a result of a love affair. Crates' wife herself was like another Crates. But we are talking about ordinary marriages, not affected by special considerations. We do not find marriage, under normal circumstances, is a preferred action for a Cynic."

"How then will he keep society going?"

For heaven's sake, who benefits the society more? Those who produce two or three snivelling brats to replace them or those who watch over humankind, examining what people do, how they live, what they take care of, and what they neglect? Who benefited Thebans more – those who give them children or Epaminondas, who died childless? [Epaminondas was a Theban general and statesman of the 4th Century BCE. He led the Greek city-state of Thebes to freedom, making it a prominent region in Greece.] Did Priam, who had fifty useless children, Danaus or Aeolus [kings who also had many children] contribute more to society than Homer [the author of

Iliad and *Odyssey* who had neither a home nor a family]? Their life as poet or general was considered sufficient contribution to exempt them from marrying and bringing up children. Shouldn't the kingship of a Cynic be considered as sufficient contribution as well?

Perhaps we don't understand the greatness of [the Cynic philosopher] Diogenes or fully appreciate his character. We rather think of Cynics as they are now: "Dogs who beg at the table and hang about the gate" [*Iliad, 22.* As translated by Robert Dobbin], who have nothing in common with the founders except perhaps farting in public. Otherwise, we would not be surprised or disappointed if a Cynic does not marry, or have children. Consider him, my friend, as the father of humankind; every man is his son and every woman is his daughter. It is in his nature to approach everyone and take care of everyone. Or do you think that he is meddlesome enough to denounce everyone he meets? No, he does it as a father, as a brother, as a servant of our common parent, God.

A Cynic is always engaged in public affairs

Go on and ask me if a Cynic will engage in public affairs. Tell me, you fool, what public affair are you looking for other than the one he is engaged in right now? Or should he come forward and give speeches to his fellow citizens about revenues and taxes when his business is to talk to the entire humankind – not about debits and credits or war and peace – but about happiness and unhappiness, good fortune and bad, slavery and freedom? You are asking me if someone will engage in public affairs when he is already engaged in it in such a big way. Ask me, too, whether he will accept public office. I will tell you, "What office, you fool, is greater than the one he has now?"

A Cynic's body, however, should be in good shape. His philosophy will not carry much conviction if it comes from a sickly, thin, and pale body. It is not enough for him to prove to ordinary people, through constancy of his mind, that it is possible to be good and noble without the material things they value. He also has to show, by his body, that a plain and simple outdoor life is wholesome: "See, both I and my body testify." This was so with Diogenes. He walked about with radiant health and would draw the attention of the crowd by it. But a Cynic who aroused pity seems like a beggar. People avoid him and are offended by him. He should not be dirty and thus scare away people. Even his ruggedness should be clean and engaging.

A Cynic is sharp and witty

A Cynic should also have great natural charm and sharpness of mind, so he can always respond readily and correctly to every situation. (Otherwise, he is just a windbag.) Thus, when someone asked Diogenes, "Are you the Diogenes who does not believe that gods exist?" Diogenes replied, "How can you say that when I know gods despise you?"

Again, when Alexander the Great stood over him while he was sleeping and recited [Homer's line from Iliad],

"To sleep the whole night does not fit with the man who counsels."

Diogenes, still half-asleep, answered him [with the next line in Iliad]

"One who has the people in his care should be watchful about many things."

A Cynic is pure

Above all, his governing principle should be purer than the Sun; otherwise he must necessarily be a gambler, and a man of no principles because he lectures others while he himself is guilty of some vice. This is how it stands: Even corrupt kings and tyrants, because they have weapons and bodyguards, can reprimand and punish wrongdoers. A Cynic derives the same authority of weapon and bodyguards through his conscience. He knows he has watched over others and worked on their behalf. His sleep is pure, and he wakes up even purer. His thoughts were of a friend and servant of the gods and he shares in the governance of gods and is ready to say under all conditions,

"Lead me Zeus; and thou, O Destiny,"

And,

"If this what pleases the gods, so be it."

Why then, should such person not speak boldly to his brothers? To his children? In a word, his own relations?

Therefore, such a person is neither a busybody nor med-dler. He is not concerning himself with other people's business, but his own when he looks after the common welfare. If you don't agree, then, by your logic, a general is interfering if he inspects, reviews, watches over his soldiers, and punishes the disorderly

If, however, you criticize others when you're hiding a cake under your arm, let me ask you: Wouldn't you ra-ther go off into a corner and eat up what you have stolen? What do *you* have to do with other people's affairs? Who are you anyway? The bull in the herd? The queen of the hive? Show me the proof of your authority, such as the queen bee has from nature. If you are a drone and claim to be the king of bees, don't you think your fellow-citi-zens will throw you out, just as bees do the drones?

A Cynic protects what is his own, surrenders what is not to others

Besides, the Cynic must have so much patient endurance that most people would consider him unresponsive like a stone. [As far as he is concerned,] no one insults him, no one beats him, no one hurts him, because he has sur-rendered his body to others to abuse as they like. He knows that whatever is inferior must yield to what is su-perior. Physically, the body is inferior to the crowd, which is stronger in that respect. He does not enter into contests that he cannot win, and so he immediately gives up what is not his own, lays no claim to his slavish body.

But when it comes to matters of choice and proper use of impressions, you will see he has so many eyes that you would say that Argos is blind by comparison. [In Greek mythology, Argos or Argus Panoptes is a giant with many eyes.] Does he prematurely assent? Is his impulse ever thoughtless? Is his desire ever frustrated? Does he ever incur aversion? Is his purpose ever unrealized? Is he fault-finding, envious, or does he humiliate himself? It is for these things he devotes all his attention and effort. As for the rest, he lies back and yawns and is wholly at peace. No one can rob him of his choice.

But, of his body? Yes. Of his property? Yes. Of honours and offices? Yes. What does he care for these things? So, when someone tries to frighten him with the loss of these things, he says, "Go and look for children, to whom masks are frightening. But *I* know they are made of earthenware and there's nothing inside them."

Be aware of your resources and limitations

This, then, is the enterprise which you are thinking of pursuing. So, I ask you, in the name of God, put off your decision. Look first at your resources. Remember what Hector said to Andromache: "Go into the house and weave. War will be the concern of all men, mine in particular." [Homer's *Iliad,* paraphrased.] He was so aware of his own resources and her incapacity.

Think about this

Plan carefully, know your limits, be reasonable. Discourses II.22.53. Epictetus [RD]

Move Your Audience to Examine Their Lives

Key ideas of this discourse

1. First decide what you want to be and then act accordingly.
2. We use standards for our behaviour. There are two such standards: A general standard that tells us how to behave like human beings and a specific standard that applies to your chosen occupation and choices.
3. To teach philosophy, you must practice it first.
4. A true philosopher is not a show-off. He does not seek praise from the audience.
5. A philosopher's job is to move his audience to examine their lives.

First decide what you want to be and then act accordingly

First, tell yourself what you want to be and go ahead and act accordingly in all that you do. We find this to be the practice in almost every field. Athletes decide first what kind of athlete they want to be and train accordingly. If they decide to be a long-distance runner, it means one particular diet, walking, massaging, and certain specific workouts. If they decide to be a sprinter, these are all somewhat different. If it is pentathlete you want to be, it is even more different. You will find the same in arts. If you are a carpenter, you'll undergo one kind of training; if a blacksmith, a different kind of training. If you do not follow a standard in each one of your actions, you will be acting at random. If we follow an improper standard, we will fail completely.

There are two action standards: one general and one specific

There are two standards of action: one general and one particular. First of all, we must act like human beings. What does it include? Don't act like sheep, however gentle you are, or like a violent wild beast. Next, there's the particular standard that relates to your chosen occupation and choice. A musician must act like a musician, a carpenter like a carpenter, a philosopher like a philosopher, the orator like an orator. Therefore, when you say, "Come and hear me lecture," first see that you are not acting without fixed purpose. Then, when you find your standard, make sure it is the right one. Do you want to educate or be praised? Right away you get the answer, "What do I care for praise from the crowd?" An excellent answer. The same is true of musicians as musicians and mathematicians as mathematician – they do not care about praise.

You cannot teach what you don't practice

You want to benefit others, don't you? In what? Tell us, so we'll go running to the lecture theatre as well. Now, can someone benefit others if he has not received benefits himself? No, not any more than a person who is not a carpenter can give lessons in carpentry or a person who is not a cobbler can give lessons on making footwear. Do you want to know if you received any benefit? Show me your judgments, philosopher.

"What is the goal of desire?" Never to fail in getting what it wants.

"And of aversion?" Not falling into what it doesn't want.

Now, are you achieving these goals? Tell me the truth. Because, if you lie, I'll tell you that the other day, when your audience was somewhat cold and did not applaud, you went away dejected. On another day, when the audience did applaud, you went asking everybody:

"How did you think I did?"

"It was marvellous, I swear by my life."

"How did I render that particular part?"

"Which?"

"Where I described Pan and the Nymphs."

"It was superb!"

Instead, we seek praise from others

After all this, are you trying to tell me that regarding desire and aversion, you act in line with nature? Go away and trying telling it to someone else who might believe you! Didn't you, just the other day, praise so-and-so contrary to your honest opinion? Weren't you flattering a senator? Would you want your children to behave like him?

"God forbid!"

"Then why did you praise him and sweet-talk him?"

"He's a gifted young man who enjoys listening to discourses."

"How do you know?"

"He admires me."

"Ah that's proof enough!"

What do you suppose is going on? Isn't it true that these are the same people who secretly despise you? So, someone who has never done – or even considered doing – a good thing finds a philosopher who tells him, "You're a genius, honest and unspoilt." What does he think to himself except that, "This man wants some favour or another from me"? So, tell me, what sign of great talent has he shown? After all, he has been with you for some time, he has listened to your discussions and heard your lectures. Has he gained more self-control? Has he paid regard to himself? Has he realized his faults? Has he given up his conceit? Has he begun to look for a teacher?

"He has."

"One who would teach him how to live? No, fool. Only for someone who would teach him how he should talk. It is for this he admires you."

Listen to him now and hear what he says. "This man is much more artistic in his writing. Much better than Dio." This is very different. He does not say, "This man is self-respecting, trustworthy, and calm." And, even if he did say that, I would ask, "Since this man is trustworthy, tell me, what does it mean exactly?" And, if he could not say, I would have added, "Understand what words mean before you speak." While you are in this sorry state, eager for admirers and counting the number of your audience, do you wish to benefit others?

"Today I had a much greater audience."

"Yes, huge."

"Five hundred, I guess."

"Nonsense. Make it a thousand."

"Dio never had so large an audience."

"How could he?"

"Yes, it was a sophisticated audience. They are clever in catching rhetorical points."

"Beauty, sir, can move a mountain."

These are the words of a philosopher for you! Here's the nature of a man who wants to benefit humankind! This is a man who has listened to reason, has read the Socratic discourses as coming from Socrates, not as though it came from [rhetoricians] Lysias or Isocrates.

"I often wondered by what arguments ...."
"No, 'by what *argument*' reads better.'"

We miss the main points philosophers like Socrates tried to teach us

You read them as you would music-hall songs. Because, if you had read them properly, you wouldn't care about that, but would care more for this:

"Anytus and Meletus can kill me, but they cannot harm me."

[Socrates, as quoted from Plato's *Apology*]

"I've always been the kind of person who attends only to arguments that seem best upon inspection, even if I have to neglect my own affairs."

[Socrates, as quoted from Plato's *Crito*]

That's why no one ever heard him say,

"I know something, and I teach it."

[Socrates denied knowing anything and did not volunteer to teach or accept money.]

Instead, he would send different people to different instructors. So, people came to him to be introduced to philosophers. But you probably think that, as he went along with them, he would say, "Come and listen to me speak at the house of Quadratus." [It was customary during Epictetus' time for distinguished scholars to be invited to speak in one's house.]

"Why should I listen to you? Do you want to show me how cleverly you have put the words together? So you do. But what good does it do to you?"

"You are supposed to praise me."

"What do you mean by praise? Shout, 'Bravo!' or, 'Marvellous!' All right, I will shout it. But if praise is seen as good by philosophers, then, how can I praise you? Teach me that it is a good thing and I will praise you."

"Are you saying that we should take no pleasure in listening to fine words?"

"Of course not. I take pleasure in listening to a harp. But is that any reason for me to get up and play the harp?"

Hear what Socrates says to his judges:

"It would not be fitting for me to appear before you at my age and formulate phrases like an immature youth." [Socrates, as quoted from Plato's *Apology*]

"Like an immature youth," he says. For it is indeed an exquisite thing – this art of choosing words and putting them together and then reciting them in public; and then, in the middle of the discourse saying, "By God, there are not many people who can understand this!"

A philosopher's job is to move the audience to action, not to seek praise

But does a philosopher invite people to a lecture? Like the Sun which draws nourishment to itself, a philosopher attracts people in need of help. What doctor would ever invite patients, so he can treat them? (Although, now I hear that in Rome even doctors advertise for patients. In my time, they were called in by patients.)

"I invite you to come and hear how unwell you are:

- You take care of everything except what you should;
- You don't know good from evil; and
- You are unfortunate and unhappy."

A charming invitation! Yet, unless a philosopher produces this effect through his speech, it is lifeless and so is the philosopher. [Epictetus' teacher] Rufus used to say, "If you find leisure time to praise me, my speech was a failure." He would speak in such a way as to make everyone who heard him suppose that someone had informed on him. Such was his understanding of how people behave that he vividly placed each man's private fault in front of him.

Do not try to show off

The school of a philosopher is a hospital. When you leave, you should leave in pain, not pleasure. You were not healthy when you came in. You had a dislocated shoulder, or an abscess, or a fistula, or a headache. So, am I supposed to sit down with you and recite with your pretty thoughts and reflections so you go away praising me, but with the same dislocated shoulder, the same abscess, the same fistula, or the same headache that you came with? And is it for this that young people should travel abroad, leaving their parents, friends, relations, and possessions behind, so they can say, "Bravo!" as you deliver your clever phrases? Is this what [philosophers like] Socrates, Zeno and Cleanthes did?

"Well, isn't there a right style for discourses and conversations?"

"Who denies that? Just as there is a style for disproof and a style for instruction. But whoever included a fourth style – the style for showing off?"

What is the style for discourses? The one that enables you to show one or more people the conflicts they are involved in and how they are involved in everything except what they should care for: they want what would make them happy, but they are looking in the wrong place. To achieve this, do we really need to set a thousand chairs, invite people, wear a fancy robe as a speaker, walk up to the podium and describe the death of Achilles? For heaven's sake, stop doing all such things that would discredit noble words. There's nothing more inspiring than a speaker who shows his audience that he needs them.

But tell me, has anyone who has ever heard you reading or speaking become anxious and turned his attention upon himself as a result? Or, said as he left, "That philosopher touched a nerve there. I can't continue to behave the way I do"? No, instead of this, if you really perform well, one person says to another, "That part about Xerxes was well put." And the other person says, "I liked his description of [the war of] Thermopylae better."

Is that what it means to listen to a philosopher?

Think about this

What people want is what conduces to happiness; but they look for it in the wrong place. Discourses II.23.34. Epictetus [RD]

Train to Be at Home
Wherever You Are

Key ideas of this discourse

1. *When we leave our place or the people we love, we long for them*
2. *But all things are impermanent. To wish them to stay the same is irrational.*
3. *If someone is upset because we leave, it is because they are irrational. It is not in our power to change it.*
4. *Do what needs to be done and don't be chained to a place or to the people who you are used to.*
5. *Don't get attached to things that can be taken away from you.*
6. *Make the best use of the place you are in, with the people you are with.*

We are involved in the greatest of contests

If someone acts contrary to nature, don't think of it as an evil for you. You were not born to share in the humiliations and misfortunes of others, only in their good fortune. If someone is unhappy, remember, they are responsible for it. God made us humans to be happy and serene and, for this purpose, he gave us the resources we need, some our own, others not our own.

Whatever is subject to hindrance, removal, or compulsion is not our own, while all that is free of hindrance is. He has placed the true nature of good and bad among the things that are our own, as was fitting for one who watches over us and protects us like a father.

"But I just left so-and-so and she is heartbroken."

"Why did she consider what is not her own to be her own?"

Why did she not reflect, when she enjoyed the pleasure of your company, that you are mortal and likely to move to another place? So, she is simply paying the penalty for her foolishness. But why are you unhappy? For what purpose? Have you also failed to learn these things and, like people of no value, enjoy all that you did – the places, the people, and the way of life – as though they will last forever? Now you sit here and cry because you can no longer be with the same people and be in the same places. Yes, you deserve to be more miserable than crows and ravens, which can fly wherever they like, build their nests in different places, cross the seas, without groaning or longing for their former home.

"Yes, but they feel this way because they are not rational."

"Has God given us any reason for our misfortune and unhappiness, so we can spend our lives in perpetual misery and mourning? Or is everyone immortal, never having to leave home, but staying in one place like a plant? If anyone we know leaves home, shall we sit down and cry? If she comes back, should we dance and clap our hands like children?"

Shouldn't we, once and for all, wean ourselves and remember what we learned from philosophers, unless we listened to them merely as story-tellers? They said that this universe is just a single city; it is made of a single thing. There must be a change from time to time when one thing gives way to another, some things disappear, and other things come into being, somethings remain and other things are moved somewhere else.

Things are impermanent

The world is full of friends, first the gods and then human beings, who by nature are endeared to each other. Some must remain with one another and others leave. We should take delight in those who live with us and not be upset by those who leave. Human beings are noble minded by nature and despise things that are outside their realm of choice.

They have one additional quality: They are not rooted down or attached to the earth, but are able to move from place to place, sometimes because of necessity, sometimes merely for the sake of looking around. Something like this happened to Odysseus, *"Cities of men he saw, and learned their ways."* Before him, Heracles travelled around the entire inhabited world, "Viewing the wickedness of men he saw, and learned their ways," clearing away one while introducing the other in its place. [Quotes as translated by Robin Hard.]

Yet how many friends do you suppose he had in Thebes, Argos, or Athens? How many new friends he made while travelling around, considering that, at the right time, he would even marry and father children? And considering that he left these children as orphans without lamentation and regret? He knew that no human being is an orphan but there's a father who constantly cares for them all. Because for him it was not just idle talk that Zeus is the father of human beings, but he always thought of him as his own father, and called him so, and looked to him in all that he did. That's why he could live happily wherever he was. But it is impossible to be happy and yet crave what one doesn't have. Happiness must already have all it wants. It must resemble a person who has achieved their fill, feeling neither hungry nor thirsty.

"But Odysseus longed for his wife. He sat on a rock crying."

"Why do you always take Homer and his tales as authority for everything? If Odysseus had really cried, what was he – except an unhappy man? But what good and virtuous person is unhappy?"

[Here Epictetus is suggesting that Homer misrepresented Odysseus, since he is a good and virtuous man and so, by definition, could not have been unhappy.]

To tell the truth, the universe will be a badly managed place if Zeus doesn't take care of his citizens, making them happy like himself. No, these thoughts are unlawful and unholy. If Odysseus sat and wept, then he was not a good man. How can someone be good if he doesn't know who he is? And who can know that, if he has forgotten that things that come into being must perish, and it isn't possible for one human being to live always with another? Then what? To desire the impossible is slavish and foolish. It is the behaviour of a stranger in the world who is fighting with God with the only means available to him: his judgments.

The grief of another is not in our power

"But my mother feels sad at not seeing me."

"So why hasn't she learned these principles? I am not saying that you shouldn't make an effort to stop her from being sad, but you should not wish for something that is not absolutely in your power."

The grief of another is not in our power. But your own grief is. You will try to help others to overcome their grief as far as you are able, but not totally. Otherwise you will be fighting against nature, opposing it, and fighting against the way the universe works. The penalty for this will not be paid by your children's children, but by you personally, day and night; you'll be startled out of your dreams, when you are disturbed, fearing every message, when your peace of mind depends on the letters of others.

Someone arrives from another city. "I only hope he is not bringing bad news." Why, what harm can come to you when you were not even there? Someone arrives from yet another city. "I only hope she is not bringing bad news." Why, at this rate any place can be a source of bad news to you! Isn't it enough for you to be unhappy where you actually are? Must you be unhappy even beyond the seas and by letter? Is this the way to make everything secure?

"Yes, but if my friends over there should die?"

What does that mean except that humans are mortals and they die? Do you wish to live long and yet not see loved ones die? Don't you know, over a long period of time, many different things are bound to happen? That one person will get sick, another will get robbed, and yet another will be bullied? Such is the nature of our world and the nature of the people who are with us.

Things like heat and cold, unsuitable diet, a journey by land or sea, winds, and dangers of every kind can destroy some people, drive out some others, or make them seek help in an embassy or in a campaign.

Sit down then, get upset by all these things. Grieve. Be disappointed and be miserable. Be at the mercy of external events, not just one or two but thousands upon thousands!

Is this what you heard philosophers say? Is this what you learned? Don't you know that this life is like a campaign? One person should guard, another go on a spying mission, and yet another out to fight. All of them cannot be in the same place and it wouldn't be desirable either. But you neglect to perform the job assigned to you by the general, complain that it is hard, and don't realize how you are reducing the army to the extent you can. For, if others follow your example, no one will dig a trench, or build a fence, no one will keep watch at night, or expose himself to danger – they will all be useless as soldiers. Again, if you go on a ship as a sailor, settle down in a single spot and stick to it. If it is necessary for you to climb the mast, refuse to do it. If you have to run to the bow, refuse again. What captain will put up with you? Won't he throw you overboard like a piece of junk, nothing but a nuisance and bad example for other sailors?

Do what needs doing, don't complain

So, it is here. Everyone's life is a campaign, long and changeable. You must fulfil the duty of a soldier and do whatever your general orders you to do, sometimes even divining his wishes. For, he is no ordinary general, either in power or excellence of character. You are stationed in an imperial city, not in some miserable little place and you're a senator for life. Don't you know that such a person has little time to spend on his household affairs, but has to spend most of his time away from home giving and receiving orders, serving some official, serving in the field, or sitting as a judge? And then you tell me that you want to remain in one spot like a plant?

"Yes, it is pleasant!"

"Who is denying it? But soup is pleasant too. So is a pretty woman. Do those who go for pleasure say anything else?"

Don't you see what kind of men they are whose language you are using? This is the language of Epicurus and perverts. And while you share their opinions, are you going to quote the words of Zeno and Socrates to us? Why don't you throw these alien adornments as far away from you as possible as they don't suit you at all? What else do these fellows [Epicureans] want other than to sleep undisturbed, and when they wake up, yawn at their leisure, and wash their faces; then read and write what they like; then talk some nonsense, to the applause of their friends, no matter what they say; then go out for a walk and, after that, take a bath, eat, and go to bed – the type of bed that you would expect them to sleep in? Why should I say another word? You know what it is like.

Don't pretend to be a Stoic, if you don't have Stoic qualities

Come now, you must tell me about your style of life too – the life you hope to achieve, you who is eager for the truth and an admirer of Diogenes and of Socrates! What do *you* want to do in Athens? The things that I just described? Not anything different? Why do you call yourself a Stoic, then?

If you try to pass yourself off as a citizen of a country of which you really aren't, you will be severely punished.

Should those who claim a title and a mission as great and dignified as this [being a Stoic] go unpunished? Or is that impossible? Rather, is it an all-powerful and inescapable divine law that punishes those who are guilty of such greatest of all offences? What does this law say? "Let anyone who pretends to have qualities he doesn't have be boorish and conceited. Let him be a low-life, a slave, let him be miserable, let him envy, let him pity; in a word let him be unhappy and regretful."

Do the right thing without expectations

[*At this point, the conversation changes abruptly.*]

"What then? Would you have me pay court to so-and-so and go to his door?"

"Why not − if reason demands it for the sake your country, your family, or humanity? You are not ashamed go to a shoemaker when you need shoes, or to a vendor of vegetables when you need lettuce. Yet you are ashamed to go to the rich when you need what they have?"

"Yes, but I don't stand in awe of a shoemaker."

"Then don't stand in awe of a rich person either."

"And I don't have to flatter the vegetable vendor."

"Then don't flatter the rich person either."

"Then, how will I get what I need [from the rich person]?

"Is this what I've been telling you: 'Go as someone who will get what he wants?'. No, I said, 'Go and ask because it is the proper thing to do.'"

"Then why should I go at all?"

"You go there to fulfil your role as a citizen, as a brother and as a friend. Besides, remember that you have come to see a shoemaker, or a vegetable vendor. He has no authority over anything great or valuable, even if his prices are high. You're going there to buy lettuce. It is worth something but not that much. It is so in this case. The matter at hand is worth the trouble of going to his door. So, I will go. It's worth talking to him. So, I will talk. But is it also necessary to kiss his hands, and flatter him singing his praises? No way! That would be like paying way too much for a head of lettuce. It will not benefit me, my country, or my friends. It will destroy the good citizen and friend in me."

"But if you fail, people will think that you didn't really care to put much effort into it."

"What, have you forgotten why you went there? Don't you know that wise and good people do things because they are right and not because they look good to others? What benefit do you gain by spelling a word like Dion correctly? That of spelling it correctly."

"No further reward to be gained, then?"

"Why do you seek further rewards for a good person than doing what is wise and right? At the Olympics, you don't ask for anything further than the Olympic crown. Does it look too small and worthless to you to be good, noble, and happy?

Don't long for the past

Since you have been introduced to this great world by
the gods, it is your duty to do the work of a human being.
Do you still crave the nurses and the breast? Does the
weeping of poor silly women soften you and make you
effeminate? Don't you realize that when a man acts as a
child, the older he is, the more ridiculous he is?

"Did you see anybody in Athens, in their home?'

"Yes, I did. The man I wanted to see."

"Here as well, make up your mind and you will see
him. But don't go as someone inferior, with desire or
aversion, and you will be all right."

You will not find this result by just going or standing
at the door, but being right in your judgment – in thinking, in choosing, in desiring, and in avoiding. Then,
where is the need for flattery or gloom? Why long for the
quiet you enjoyed somewhere else, places that are familiar to you? Stay a little longer and these places will become familiar to you as well. Then, if you are mean-
spirited, weep and be miserable again when you have to
leave these too.

"How am I to show my affection, then?"

"You show it as a noble-minded person and as a fortunate person."

Reason will never ask you to humiliate yourself or be
broken-hearted, depend on others, or blame God or fellow human beings. Observing these things is how you
show your affection. However if, as a result of this

affection (however you define it), you become submissive and miserable, it does no good for you to be affectionate.

Besides, what stops you from loving someone who is bound to die, as one may have to leave you? Tell me, didn't Socrates love his children? He did, but he did so as a free man, as one who was aware that his first duty was to be a friend to the gods. That's why he succeeded in fulfilling his duties of a good man, both in defending himself and in proposing a penalty for himself, and, at an earlier time, as a member of the council or as a soldier.

But we use every excuse to be mean-spirited – some saying that it is because of a child, others because of their mother and yet others because of their brothers. We should not be unhappy because of someone else, but we should be happy for all, most of all for God, who made us for this purpose.

Be at home wherever you are

What! Was there anyone at all whom Diogenes didn't love? Was he not so gentle and kind-hearted that he gladly took upon himself so many troubles and physical hardships for the common good of humanity?

"But in what way did he show his love?"

"By taking good care of others while being obedient to God, as a servant of God,"

That's why the whole world, not any particular place, was his country. When he was taken prisoner, he didn't long for Athens and for his friends and acquaintances

STOIC TRAINING • 157

there. Instead, he befriended the pirates and tried to reform them. Later, when he was sold into slavery, he lived
in Corinth just as he had previously lived at Athens. If he
had gone off to the [remote mountainous region of] Per-
rhaebians, he would have done exactly the same.

"This is how one achieves freedom. That's why he
used to say, "Ever since [the founder of Cynicism] Antisthenes set me free, I stopped being a slave."

"How did Antisthenes set him free?"

"Listen to Diogenes himself: 'Antisthenes taught me
what is mine and what is not mine. Property isn't mine;
relations, family, friends, reputation, familiar places,
conversation with others aren't mine either.'"

"What, then, is yours?"

"Power to deal with external impressions."

He showed me that I have this power, free from all
compulsion. No one can obstruct me, or force me to deal
with impressions in any other the way than I choose to.
Who still holds power over me? Philip? Alexander?
Perdiccas? Or the King of Persia? How could they? Only
when you are first overpowered by things, can you be
overpowered by another human being."

So, if you don't allow yourself to be overpowered by
pleasure, or by suffering, or by fame or by wealth; if, at
the time of your choice, you are prepared to let go of
your body if someone threatens it, how can you ever be
a slave? To whom are you subordinate?

But if Diogenes had continued to live pleasantly in
Athens, hooked on the way of life there, his life could be
controlled by anybody. Anyone who was stronger than

him could cause him grief. You can imagine how he would have flattered the pirates to make them sell him to an Athenian, so he could see the beautiful Piraeus, the Long Walls, and the Acropolis again.

"And what sort of a person would you be when you see them?"

"A miserable slave."

"And what good would that do to you?"

"No, not as a slave, but as a free man."

"Show me in what way you're free. Someone, whoever he may be, gets hold of you and takes you away from the lifestyle you are accustomed to and says, 'You are my slave because I have the power to prevent you from living the way you want. I have the power to set you free or humble you. Whenever I choose you may be cheerful again and go off to Athens in good spirits.' What do you say to this man? What are you going to offer him to set you free? Isn't it true that you don't even dare to look at him in the face but, avoiding all arguments, beg him to release you?"

Man, you might as well go to prison happily, hurrying off even before they arrest you to be taken there. Are you reluctant to live in Rome and long for Greece? And, when you have to die, will you come crying to us once more because you'll never see Athens again? Or that you won't be able to walk around the Lyceum?

Is it for this that you travelled abroad? Is it for this that you are looking for someone who might do you good? Do good in what way? In analysing syllogisms easily and dealing with hypothetical arguments methodically? Is this the reason why you left your brother, country, friends and family, to be able to go back home with this kind of knowledge?

So, you did not travel abroad to gain firmness of mind; it wasn't to achieve peace of mind; it wasn't to become free from harm and thus stop blaming or finding fault with anyone; and it wasn't to make it impossible for anyone to harm you and be able to keep your social relationships without being obstructed?

A fine trade-off, indeed! To bring back home syllogisms, arguments with hypothetical and equivocal premises!

Yes, if you see fit, you should go sit in the marketplace, put up a sign like medicine peddlers do. Shouldn't you deny that you know even what you've learned, so you don't bring a bad reputation to the philosophical doctrines? What harm has philosophy ever done to you? What wrong has Chrysippus done that you should try to prove by your actions that his efforts were useless? Weren't the troubles at home enough to cause you sorrow and distress? Do you have to travel abroad to add to them?

And when you gain new friends and acquaintances, you will find new reasons to be miserable. You will get attached to the new place as well. So, what's the purpose for your living? To pile sorrow upon sorrow and make yourself miserable? And then you tell me this is affection? What kind of affection is this? If natural affection is good, it cannot result in any evil. If it is evil, I want to have nothing to do with it. I am born for what is good and what belongs to me, not for what is evil.

How to train properly

"How do you train for this properly, then?"

First and foremost, the highest and the principal form of training, which stands at the entrance is this. When you become attached to something, don't think it cannot be taken away from you. Rather it is like a cup made of glass or ceramics. If it breaks, remember that is its nature and you won't be troubled. So, it is here too. When you kiss your child, your brother, your friend, don't let your imagination run wild unchecked. Hold it back and restrain it like those who stand behind the generals riding in triumph and keep reminding them that they are mortals. [This refers to the ancient practice of a slave riding behind a victorious general to ward off the evil eye. While the general was being acclaimed, the people would say "Look behind you. Remember that you are a mortal."] In the same way, you too should remind yourself that what you love is mortal. What you love is not your own. It has been given to you for the time being, not permanently, not forever. Rather it is given to you like fig or a bunch of grapes, for a particular season of the year. If you crave for it in the winter, you are a fool.

So, if you long for your son or friend at a time when they are no longer given to you, know that you are longing for a fig in winter. For as winter is to a fig, so is everything that arises from the general order of things in relation to what is destroyed.

From now on, whenever something delights you, call to mind the opposite impression. What harm is there if you whisper to yourself as you are kissing your child, "Tomorrow you'll die"? Or to your friend, "Tomorrow you'll go abroad, or I will, and we will never see each other again."?

"But these are words that can bring bad luck."

"Yes, but so are some ritual chants. I don't mind, as long as they do only good."

Do you call anything bad luck except what indicates something bad for us? Cowardice, meanness of spirit, sorrow, and shamelessness – all these are words of bad luck. And yet, we should not avoid using them, if they will protect us from the things themselves.

Are you telling me that any word that signifies some process of nature is bad luck? Is it bad luck for corn to be harvested because corn is destroyed? Is it bad luck for leaves to fall, or for a fresh fig to turn into a dried one, or for grapes to turn into raisin? All these things involve changes from their former state to a new and different one. It is not destruction but an orderly management and organization. Travelling abroad is like that, a small change. Death is like that, a big change, a change from what is into what it *presently* is not (rather than what is not).

"So, I won't exist anymore?"

You won't exist, but something else that the world needs will. You did not come into being when you wanted to, but when the world had a need for you. Therefore, a wise and good person, keeping in mind who she is, and where she came from and who created her, thinks about one thing only: how to fulfil her place in a disciplined manner, remaining obedient to God.

"Is it your will that I continue to live? I'll live as a free and noble person as you wish me to be. You have made me free from hindrance in all things that are my own. Now you don't have any further need for me? May all be well with you. I have remained here so far only because of you and no other. Now I obey you and leave.

"How do you leave?"

"Again, as you wish. As a free person, as your servant, taking note of your commands and your prohibitions. But so long as I remain in your service, what would you like me to be? An official, a private citizen, a general, a teacher, or the head of a household? Whatever place or position you give me, as Socrates says, I'll die a thousand times rather than abandon it."

Where do you want me to be? In Rome, Athens, Thebes, or Gyara? Only remember me there. If you send me to a place where it is impossible to live in accordance with nature, I shall depart from this life. Not out of disobedience to you, but in the belief that you are giving me the signal to leave. I'm not abandoning you, heaven forbid! But I realize you have no further need for me. But if you give a life in accordance with nature, I will not look for a place other than where I am or look for company other than who I am with now.

Remember and rehearse these thoughts

Have these thoughts ready at hand, day or night. Write them, read them, and discuss them both with yourself and others and say, "Can you give me some help in this?" Go to different people. If something undesirable should happen, the thought that "this is not unexpected" should lighten the burden. It is no small thing to say on every such occasion, "I knew I fathered a mortal," [An expression at that time indicating courage while facing an unfortunate condition.] That's what you'll say, and furthermore, "I knew that I was mortal," "I knew I was likely to leave home," "I knew I could be deported," or "I knew that I could be thrown in prison." Then, if you think about these events and where they came from, you will remember that they are all outside your choice and therefore not your own. So, what does it matter to you?

Accept reality as it is at any time

Then comes the comes the main question: "Who sent it?" If it was the ruler, the general, the state, or the law of the state, let it be so, because you must obey the law in everything. Later on, if your imagination still bothers you (after all, this is not under your control), fight against it with reason, defeat it, don't allow it to gain strength. Don't let it go on to the next stage picturing whatever it wants, in the way it wants it. If you are in Gyara, don't picture how it was in Rome, what pleasures you enjoyed there and what pleasures await you there if you go back.

Since Gyara is where you are now, you should live boldly there, as is proper for someone who lives there. And if you are in Rome, don't imagine the way of life in Athens, but think only about how best live where you are.

Finally, in place of all other pleasures, think of the ones that come from the awareness that you are obeying God and that you are playing the part of a good and excellent person, not just in words but in deeds as well. How great it would be to be able to tell yourself,

"Now I am actually doing what others only talk about solemnly in their schools, things that appear paradoxical. Others are just sitting and talking about my virtues, enquiring about me, and singing my praises. God wanted me to show proof of all this through my actions. He wanted to know if he has the right kind of soldier, the right kind of citizen in me, so he can present me to others as a witness about things that are outside our choice and say to them: 'See, your fears and desires are baseless. They are against reason. Don't look for what is good for you outside yourselves. Look for it within you or you'll never find it.' That's why God brings me here at one time and there at another; shows me to humanity as one who is poor, one with no official position, one who is sick; he sends me off to a remote place and puts me in prison. It's not because he hates me. Heaven forbid! Who hates the best of his servants? It isn't because he neglects me either. He does not neglect even the least of his servants. Rather, he is training me and making me his witness in front of others. When he has chosen me for this purpose, do I still care where I am? Or what people say about me?

Shouldn't I be paying full attention to what he says and what he orders me to do?"

Now if you keep such thoughts at hand, and rehearse them over and over again in your mind, and keep them ready for use, you won't need anyone to encourage you or to strengthen you. You are not disgraced by not having anything to eat but by not having reason that is strong enough to protect you from fear and grief. If, one day, you achieve freedom from fear and grief, will any bully or his sidekicks or other powerful people be anything you? If someone is awarded a high position, would you be envious? Would you envy people offering sacrifices upon taking office when you're appointed by God for a very important office?

Just don't make a display of it and don't boast about it. Prove it by your conduct. Even if no one notices, be content to live in health and happiness yourself.

Think about this

Dishonour, in truth, doesn't consist in not having enough to eat, but in not having reason enough to preserve you from fear and distress. Discourses III.24.116. Epictetus

Train to Achieve Your Goal

Key ideas of this discourse

1. *We are involved in the greatest contest. The goal is to achieve happiness and good fortune.*
2. *Even if you fail, nothing will stop you from coming back to enter the contest again.*
3. *But do not make it a habit of failing. It will only breed more failure.*

We are involved in the greatest of contests

Consider the things you set out to achieve. You achieved some of these and didn't achieve others. Some of these are pleasant to remember and others are painful to remember. If possible, try also to recover things that have slipped from your grasp.

If you are involved in the greatest of contests, you must not pull back but be prepared to take blows. The contest we are involved in is not like wrestling or a sport with no rules. For, in those contests, winning or losing does not decide whether you are a person of the highest worth or little and, by God, whether you are happy or miserable. No, this is a contest for good fortune and happiness itself.

Even if you are beaten, you can re-enter the game when you're ready again

What follows then? In this contest, even if we give in for the time being, no one can stop us from coming back to fight again. It is not necessary to wait for another four years as you do for the Olympics either. As soon as you recover your strength, and show the same enthusiasm, you can re-enter the contest. If you fail again, you can re-enter again. Once you win the contest one day, it will be as though you never gave in.

But don't make failure a habit

But, don't make it a habit of being happy to repeat the process over and over again. You might end up like a bad athlete, to be beaten again and again in the whole cycle, just like quails that run away.

"I'm overcome by the impression of a pretty girl."

"What of it? Didn't you overcome something like that just the other day?"

"I feel like disparaging someone. Didn't I have a go at someone the other day?"

"You are talking as though it had no cost to you. It is like a patient, when asked not to take a bath by a doctor, responding, 'But, didn't I take a bath just the other day?' Then the doctor may respond, 'How did you feel after the bath – did you suffer a fever or a headache?' So, when you disparaged someone the other day, did you not feel like an ill-natured person? Weren't you talking non-sense? Didn't you feed this habit by citing the examples of your own previous actions?"

Why do you then talk about what you did recently? You should have remembered them in the same way slaves remember the blows they've received – to avoid repeating the same mistakes. But these two cases are not the same. With slaves' memory it is the pain that brings back the memory. What pain, what punishment followed your faults? And when did you ever develop the habit of avoiding bad actions?

Think about this

The contest that lies before us is not in wrestling or the pankration ... no, this is a contest for good fortune and happiness itself. Discourses III.25. Epictetus [CG/RH]

Train to Confront
the Fear of Death

Key ideas of this discourse

1. *There is no shame in anything that is not of your making.*
2. *You should never fear the future. You will always have resources to cope with whatever happens.*
3. *The worst thing that can happen is death. But the source of all evils is not death, but the fear of death.*
4. *Train yourself to face the fear of death.*

We are involved in the greatest of contests

Aren't you ashamed to be more cowardly and dishonourable than a runaway slave? When they run off, how do they leave their masters? On what estate or servants can they rely? Don't they steal just a little to last them for the first few days, and then make their way around by land

and sea, devising one plan after another to keep themselves fed? And which of them ever died of hunger?

But you tremble and lie awake at night for fear that you may lack the necessities of life. Miserable man, are you too blind to see where such lack of necessities will lead? Just to the same place as a fever or a stone that drops on your head – to death. Haven't you often said so to your friends, read or written things of this nature? How often have you boasted that you are fairly confident at least as far as death is concerned?

"Yes, but family will also starve."

"What of it? Will their hunger take them in any other direction than yours?"

Is it not the same road that leads below? Isn't the world below the same? Aren't you willing to look at that place, with courage sufficient to face every necessity and want, where even the wealthiest, holders of high offices including kings and tyrants must finally go? It may well be that you will go there hungry while they will go with indigestion and drunkenness.

There is no shame in anything that is not of your making

Is it not easy to find a beggar who is old? Or one who is extremely old? But although they are cold by night and by day, and lie outside on the ground, and have no food beyond the bare essentials, they have reached a state where it is almost impossible for them to die. And yet, here you are physically fit and have hands and feet – are you so very afraid of starving? Can't you fetch water, or write, or take children to school or be somebody's door-keeper?

"But it is shameful to be reduced to that level."

"Learn therefore what is shameful. Call yourself a philosopher only after that. At present you shouldn't even allow anyone to call you a philosopher."

Is anything shameful to you, if it is not your own doing, for which you are not responsible, which has come to you uninvited, like a headache or fever? If your parents were poor, or if they were rich but left their property to others, gave you no help during their lifetime, is there anything shameful for you in that? Is that what you learned from philosophers? Have you not learned that what is shameful is blameworthy and only what is blameworthy deserves blame? And whom do you blame for something that's not your own doing, and which you did not bring upon yourself?

Well, did you bring about this situation? Did you make your father what he is? Is it in your power to reform him? Is this power given to you? What then? Wish for what is not given to you and be ashamed if you don't get it? Is this what you learned while studying philosophy – to look to other people but hope for nothing from yourself? Well then, weep and whimper and eat in fear that you may have no food tomorrow. Tremble about your help-ers fearing that they will steal from you, run away, or die. Live this way and never stop doing it. You have come to philosophy in name only. You have discredited its principles by showing them to be useless and good for nothing for those who practice them!

Your objectives should be stability, serenity, and peace of mind

Never have you desired stability, serenity, peace of mind. Never have you approached anyone for that purpose, but only learn about syllogisms. You never tested an impression for yourself, "Am I able to bear it or not? What can I expect next?" As if everything is safe and sound for you, you've been devoting your attention to a topic that should actually come at the end – immutability or you how you may be unassailable. Unassailable in what? [In your case,] your cowardice, your meanness of spirit, your admiration of the rich, your failure to get what you desire and your failure to avoid what you want to avoid. These are the things that you have been so anxious to secure!

Shouldn't you have started by getting something from reason, and then try to make that secure? Have you seen anyone building a cornice without having a wall to build it around? What kind of doorkeeper can you place on guard where there isn't any door? You practice the power to demonstrate. Demonstrate what? You practice to avoid being shaken by sophistic arguments. Shaken from what? Show me first what you are saving, what you are measuring, and what you are weighing. Then show me, accordingly, your scales and measure. How long will you keep measuring ashes? [Ashes here refer to externals, which are considered worthless.]

Don't get carried away by well-crafted arguments

Shouldn't you be measuring these – what makes people happy, what makes their affairs prosper for them as they wish, what makes it possible for them to blame no one, fault no one, and submit to the governing order of the universe? Show me that.

"Look, I will show you. I am going to analyse some syllogisms for you."

"That's the measuring instrument, idiot, it is not the thing that's measured."

That's why you are now being punished for what you neglected. You tremble, lie awake, consult everyone and if you don't meet with everyone's approval, you think you have been ill-advised.

Then you are afraid of going hungry, or so you think. You are not afraid of going hungry but of not having someone to cook for you, no servant to do the shopping, no one to put your shoes on, no one to dress you; no one to give you a massage, no one to follow after you so when you have undressed and stretched in a bath like someone crucified, he may massage you on this side and that. The masseurs then stand over you and say, "Move over, give me his side and you take over his head and give me his shoulder." Then, when you have returned home, you may shout out, "Is no one bringing me something to eat?" And then, "Clear the tables. Wipe them with a sponge."

You should not fear that you'll go hungry

What you are afraid of is this: that you may not be able to live the life of an invalid. To learn how healthy people live you need only look at how servants, labourers, and genuine philosophers live. Or how Socrates lived even when he had a wife and children, how Diogenes lived, and Cleanthes lived while having to study and draw water at the same time. [Cleanthes was the second scholarch or head of the Stoic school. He was so poor that he attended Zeno's school during the day and worked as a gardener at night to support himself.] If this is what you want, you'll find it everywhere and you can live with complete confidence. Confidence in what? In the only things in which we *can* have confidence – that which is reliable, free from hindrance, and cannot be taken away; in short, your own moral choice.

Why have you made yourself so useless and good for nothing that no one is willing to take you into his home, no one is willing to take care of you? When an undamaged and useful tool is thrown out, anyone who finds it will take it with him and count it a gain. But not when he picks *you* up. Everyone will count you a loss. You are not even as useful as a dog or a cock. Why do you care to go on living, if that's the kind of person you are?

Does any good person fear that he will go hungry?

Neither the blind nor the lame go hungry. Will a good person?

A good soldier doesn't fail to find someone to employ him and pay him. Neither do good workers and shoemakers. Will a good person?

The worst thing that can happen is death

Does God neglect his own creatures, his own servants, his witnesses — the only people he uses as examples to the uneducated to prove that he exists and governs the universe well, does not neglect human affairs, and nothing bad ever happens to a good person, either in life or in death?

"Yes, but what if he fails to provide me with food?"

"What else? Like a good general, he is signalling you to withdraw."

I came into this world when it pleased him and leave it again at his pleasure. While I lived, it was my job to sing hymns of his praise to myself or to others, one or many. He has not given me much, nothing in abundance. He doesn't want me to live luxuriously. He didn't grant that to his own son Heracles either. Someone else ruled over Argos and Mycenae, while Heracles just followed orders, worked hard, and completed his work. Eurystheus, who had the title of king, did not rule over Argos and Mycenae either, since he didn't even rule over himself, while Heracles was ruler and governor of all land and sea. He purged the world of lawlessness and injustice and introduced reverence and justice. And this he achieved naked and alone.

Again, when Odysseus was shipwrecked and cast ashore, did his helpless condition make him miserable? Was his spirit broken? No. How did he approach the young girls to ask for food – something that is thought to be shameful for one person to ask of another? "Like a mountain-bred lion." [Homer, *Odyssey*]

In what did he trust? Not reputation, nor money, nor offices, but in his own strength – his judgements about which things are under our control and which aren't. These are the only things that make us free, that make us free from hindrance, that raise up the head of those who are humiliated, and make them look into the faces of the rich and of the tyrants with level eyes. This is what philosophy can offer. But you will not leave here with confidence, but with trembling about such insignificant things like clothes and silver plate. Miserable man! Is that how you have wasted your time up until now?

"But what if I get sick?"

"You will bear it well."

"Who will care for me?"

"God and your friends."

"My bed is hard."

"Lie on it like a human being."

"I won't have a suitable house."

"Then you'll fall ill in an unsuitable house."

"Who will prepare my food?"

"Those who prepare for others. You will be ill like Manes." [Likely, the name of a slave.]

"How will my illness end?"
"What else but death?"

The source of all evils is not death, but the fear of death

Why don't you realize then that the source of all human evils, mean-spiritedness, and cowardice is not death itself but the fear of death? Train yourself to face this. You should direct all your reasoning, all your studies, and all your exercises towards this end. Then you will know that it is the only way for you to achieve freedom.

Think about this

[The] source of all human evils, and of mean-spiritedness and cowardice is not death, but rather the fear of death. Discourses III.26.38. Epictetus [CH/RH]

ABOUT THE AUTHOR

Dr Chuck Chakrapani has been a long-term, but embarrassingly inconsistent, practitioner of Stoicism. He is the president of Leger Analytics, Chief Knowledge Officer of The Blackstone Group in Chicago and a Distinguished Visiting Professor at Ryerson University.

Chuck has written books on several subjects over the years which include research methods, statistics, and investment strategies. His personal website is Chuck-Chakrapani.com

His books on Stoicism include *Unshakable Freedom*, *A Fortunate Storm*, *The Good Life Handbook* (a rendering of Epictetus' Enchiridion), *Stoic Foundations*, and *Stoic Choices*.

ALSO BY THE AUTHOR

Stoic Foundations

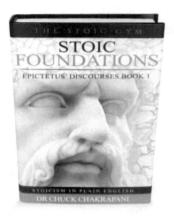

Stoic Foundations is the plain English version of Discourses Book 1 by the eminent Stoic philosopher Epictetus.
It revolves around 10 themes which are also repeated in other places throughout Discourses. These are:

- Concern yourself with only what is in your power
- Be content to let things happen as they do
- Your thinking, not the externals, drives your behaviour
- Do not place value on external things
- Don't give in to your anger or animal instincts
- You can handle anything; always act your best
  Learn to think properly and logically
- Practice, not knowledge, results in progress
- Only you can make you happy

Available from Amazon.com and other online bookstores now

Stoic Choices

Stoic Choices is the plain English version of Discourses Book 2 by the eminent Stoic philosopher Epictetus.

It revolves around 10 themes which are also repeated in other places throughout Discourses. Here are some of the choices discussed in this book:

- What should you act upon: External things or internal things?
- When should you choose to be confident and when to be cautious in making decisions?
- What should you protect: Your inherent qualities or qualities that are not inherent to you?
- Is there a choice between knowledge and action?
- Is there a choice between knowledge and anxiety?
- Should you study logic? Why?
- Choose to be faithful.
- Choose habits that fight impressions.
- Show yourself to be worthy.
- Choose to be skilful.

Available from Amazon.com and other online bookstores now

Coming Soon

Stoic Freedom, and Stoic Inspirations

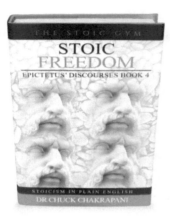 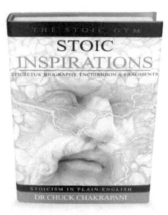

Stoic Freedom is a Plain English version of book 4 of Epictetus' Discourses. Centring around the theme of the true meaning of freedom, it is presented here by Dr Chuck Chakrapani.

Stoic Inspirations combines the Enchiridion (Epictetus' pupil Arrian's notebook summarizing his teachings) and the remaining fragments of the lost Discourses books. It completes the Stoicism in Plain English series on Epictetus from The Stoic Gym.

A Fortunate Storm

Unshakable Freedom is based on Stoic teachings.

But how did Stoicism come about?

Three unconnected events – a shipwreck in Piraeus, a play in Thebes, and the banishment of a rebel in Turkey – connected three unrelated individuals to give birth to a philosophy. It was to endure two thousand years and offer hope and comfort to hundreds of thousands of people along the way.

The Fortunate Storm is the improbable story of how Stoicism came about. You can get a FREE COPY of the e-version of this book at the link below:

http://www.TheStoicGym.com/fortunatestormfree

The Good Life Handbook

Available in Print, digital, and audio editions.

The Good Life Handbook is a rendering of Enchiridion in plain English. It is a concise summary of the teachings of Epictetus, as transcribed and later summarized by his student Flavius Arrian.

The Handbook is a guide to the good life. It answers the question, "How can we be good and live free and happy, no matter what else is happening around us?"

Ancient Stoics lived in a time of turmoil under difficult conditions. So, the solutions they found to living free was tested under very stringent conditions. For example, the author of this Handbook was a lame slave who made himself free and happy later in life by following the principles set out in this book.

Now The Stoic Gym offers *The Good Life Handbook* by Dr Chuck Chakrapani to interested readers free (Kindle and other online versions).

Download from Amazon.com now.

Unshakable Freedom

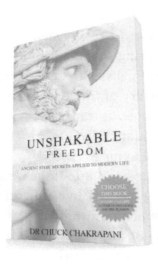

How can we achieve total personal freedom when we have so many obligations and so many demands on our time? Is personal freedom even possible?

Yes, it is possible, said the Stoics and gave us a blue print for freedom. The teachings were lost but have been rediscovered in recent times and form the basis of modern cognitive therapy.

In his new book, *Unshakable Freedom*, Dr. Chuck Chakrapani outlines the Stoic secrets for achieving total freedom, no matter who you are and what obstacles you face in life.

Using modern examples, Chuck explores how anyone can achieve personal freedom by practicing a few mind-training techniques

Available from Amazon.com and other online bookstores now

Made in United States
Troutdale, OR
11/13/2023